HOW TO
Increase YOUR
Magnetism

The Wisdom of Yogananda *series*

How to **Increase** Your **Magnetism**

Paramhansa Yogananda

THE WISDOM OF YOGANANDA, VOLUME 12

CRYSTAL CLARITY PUBLISHERS   Commerce, California

CRYSTAL CLARITY PUBLISHERS
1123 Goodrich Blvd. | Commerce, California
crystalclarity.com | clarity@crystalclarity.com
800.424.1055

ISBN   978-1-56589-349-8 (print)
ISBN   978-1-56589-644-4 (e-book)
ISBN   978-1-56589-844-8 (audiobook)
Library of Congress Cataloging-in-Publication Data (LCCN) available

Interior layout by Michele Madhavi Molloy
Series cover design by Stephanie Steyer

The *Joy Is Within You* symbol is registered by Ananda Church
of Self-Realization of Nevada County, California.

CONTENTS

PUBLISHER'S NOTE

Dear Reader,

We've all met people whose personal magnetism was exceptional — they radiated a power that enabled them to overcome their challenges and attract the right people and circumstances to help them succeed.

In the presence of magnetic people, we feel thrilling currents of energy and enthusiasm that they can apply for good — to be innovative in their work, to create wonderful art, to inspire others to positive action, and to heal their own and others' physical, emotional, mental, and spiritual suffering. In everything they undertake, they exude an irresistible energy that enables them to succeed.

What is the secret power that the world's winners possess? Can we get more of it for ourselves? Can it help us overcome our own challenges at our own level: in our work, in our relationships, in our health, and on the battlefield of daily life?

Paramhansa Yogananda promised us that the power of magnetism is well within our reach if we will learn the scientific way to increase it. He promised that, in time, the methods he taught would give us the magnetic power, as he put it, to "stand unshaken amidst the crash of breaking worlds."

He said that we already possess the tools to develop our magnetic power. They are the body, feelings, will, mind, and soul.

Yogananda introduced an approach to personal development that rests on a foundation of timeless ancient truths adapted for our present, scientifically curious age of energy-awareness.

We invite you to explore these life-changing methods, which we present here in Yogananda's own words, minimally edited and drawn from articles and lessons that he personally published.

Above all, Yogananda wants to show us how to raise our magnetism through contact with its ultimate source, in God. He taught methods for uniting our human instruments of body, heart, and mind with the Divinity that dwells eternally within us, and that is ever eager to help us find our way to greater happiness and freedom.

In divine friendship,

Crystal Clarity Publishers

Chapter 1

MAGNETIZE YOUR BODY AND MIND

BE MAGNETIC IN A POSITIVE WAY

The human soul is the image of God. It therefore has inherent within it the attractive force of Spirit. Spirit is in everything and has in Itself this drawing power, therefore all things created out of It have the individuality of Spirit and Its drawing magnetic power, though only in individualized state.

You should learn to be magnetic. There are very few people who are *really* magnetic. In developing the power of attraction lies the germ of existence.

While it is true that very few people are magnetic, nevertheless, *everybody* possesses the power of magnetism, which is the power by which you draw things to you.

We know that an ordinary magnet has a certain range and power. Small magnets draw small things. Larger magnets draw larger objects. The human magnet draws according to its power of attraction.

Magnetism is your expanding vibration.

Energy, like electricity, generates a magnetic field. And that magnetic field attracts to itself the consequences of action.

If your magnetism is not right, you will draw the wrong people or things. You must learn to develop that fine quality of magnetism by which you can draw to yourself the things that you desire and that are good for you. Most people seldom exercise their magnetic power, so naturally they do not attract anything very good.

Fear develops in an individual a malignant magnetism by which *he attracts the very object of which he is afraid*, as a magnet attracts a piece of iron or steel.

Aversion is just as strong a magnetic force as attraction. Sometimes you see whole families who do nothing but fight amongst themselves. They were enemies before [in an earlier life] — attracted together into the same home, where now they must work out their hatred at close quarters!

Hate attracts as love attracts, and what you hate you draw to yourself in a negative form.

Beware, do not bring your enemy near you nor attract his bad qualities by constantly concentrating on him through the channel of hatred.

Do not hate any nationality or anyone, for if you do, you will draw that person or nationality to yourself and you will have to come in contact with them in another life.

If you, a man, have been living on the creative-impulse plane in the present or in the past, it is quite likely that you will draw into your matrimonial circle a woman of like vibration. Like draws like.

The specific nature of the mental attitude of parents during this period [of physical union between man and woman] serves to be the magnetic force which draws the particular kind of a disembodied soul into the mother's body temple. Thoughts concentrated on physical pleasure invite sensual souls. More elevated souls refuse the invitation of degraded physical attraction. The Hindu Scriptures say that during this period a life current is generated, serving as a door for disembodied astral bodies to enter through. Elevated souls do not enter through this door of life current, if it has vibrations of low passionate mentality. They turn away at a distance. They prefer to wait rather than take a hasty re-birth in an undesirable place. So all husbands and wives should remember to cooperate spiritually, mentally, and physically in order to invite a sacred soul into the cell temple so that they may create. Married people should invoke elevated souls to come and live with them.

Today, if anyone behaves badly toward us, it is him we blame for our hurt. That we might in some way have *attracted* that hurt never enters our minds. If our "luck" turns against us, we blame anything and anyone but ourselves. Yet it is *we*, by the magnetism projected by our own karma, who drew that hurtful behavior to us, or that "rotten luck."

After passing some time in the astral world, people are then drawn back to earth, or to some other planet in the material universe, by the magnetic attraction of desire.

Plants have likes and dislikes. Metals have repulsions and affinities, just as we repulse or attract people.... The sinner is a sinner not because his parents gave him a sinful brain, but because he created it in a past life and thus attracted sinful parents.

Medical doctors would say that John inherited insanity from his insane father, but the metaphysician would say that John attracted an insane parent in this life because his soul brought back the tendency of insanity from his former life.

There is within us a magnetic force by which we attract those who have a living relationship to our magnetic power. Thus, a human being cannot attract a stone because a stone has no relation to a human being.

If a person's aura is strong, the negative consequences of his bad karma will have a greatly lessened impact on him, even though the karma must, of necessity, return to him.

In developing magnetism, you must first make up your mind as to what kind of magnetism you want.

The inner environment of man is of more importance than the outward environment. A man should first establish good within his soul, think good, and live good, and automatically he will attract a good environment.

Whatever you give out, the same will you attract.

MAGNETIZE YOUR BODY: EXERCISE, PHYSICAL AWARENESS, DIET

We must develop physical magnetism in order to have a body that is strong and conscious of itself — not to the point of vanity, but a body that obeys our command.

Overeating is bad. Fasting is very good, as it gives the stomach a rest. Your eyes and your whole body will be magnetized by the kind of food you eat.

Keep the body magnetized by right eating. Too much protein and starchy foods retain the poisons in the body. Eating freely of fruits and vegetables has a tendency to develop magnetism. Fruits have a great magnetic quality.

Raw food produces magnetism. Coconut produces lots of magnetism. Beets and spinach and lettuce are full of vitality and give you magnetism.

The magnetic diet consists of such food substitutes as sunrays and oxygen, which can be easily assimilated and converted into energy. Magnetic foods give energy more quickly than solids and liquids which are less easily converted into life force.

When you are tired or hungry, take a sunbath and you will find yourself revived and recharged with ultraviolet rays. Inhale and exhale several times outdoors or near an open window, and your fatigue will be gone. A fasting person who inhales and exhales deeply twelve times, three times a day, recharges his body with electrons and free energy from air and ether.

Practice the following exercise three times a day: Exhale slowly, counting from 1 to 6. Now, while the lungs are empty, mentally count from 1 to 6. Inhale slowly, counting from 1 to 6. Then hold the breath, counting from 1 to 6. Repeat eleven times.

Just as electricity passing through a rod made of a conductive substance electrifies it, so life force derived from oxygen charges the body battery. People who perform breathing exercises always have shining, magnetic eyes.

MAGNETIZE YOUR BODY WITH COSMIC ENERGY

Recharging the body with energy develops great magnetism.*

Diet gives partial rejuvenation, but how to tap the energy from God is the point. A time comes in your life when, no matter what you eat, nothing helps you. You grow old and nothing can stop it.

Why not learn some of the energizing methods of India? You cannot rejuvenate yourself by diet alone. There is always an inner and an outer method of rejuvenation. When a battery is dead, if you put distilled water in it,

* The appendix offers Yogananda's technique of recharging the body with Cosmic energy.

that doesn't help. The energy must be there to convert the water into energy. It is the same with the body. There comes a time when outer aids — food, air, and oxygen — will not help the body. The inner source of energy from God is then necessary.

Jesus said, "Man shall not live by bread alone, but by every word that proceedeth out of the mouth of God." Everything you eat is vibration. The air that you breathe is vibration. When you are in tune with God, you can subsist on very little food.

Behind your body wave is the vast ocean of God; behind your soul is the wisdom of God; behind your mind is the great intelligence of God; and tuning yourself in with Him, you will know that you are the child of God. Nothing shall ever destroy you. India has specialized methods of rejuvenation of body, mind, and soul. Learn from India's masters the scientific technique of inner rejuvenation.

We now come to the technique of recharging the body

battery*, by which you may learn how to draw more and more life-sustaining energy from the ether, and depend less and less upon solids, liquids, sunshine, and gases for sustenance.

Food contains a limited part of life energy, hence we can extract strength from food, but if the internal supply of life energy is exhausted, food is of no use. Therefore, we should not only sustain the human body from the outer source of energy, but should also emphasize and daily apply the method of recharging the body with energy from the *inner* source.

When God's power is flowing through you, you will be a divine magnet.

MAGNETIZE YOUR MIND

Those who are accustomed to being calm, attract *more* calmness and serenity, while those who are little calm find their calmness easily disturbed when restlessness invades. Unspiritual habits entirely destroy the power of

* You will find it in the appendix at the end of this book.

weak spiritual habits. Habits of thought are mental magnets which draw unto themselves specific objects relative to the kind and quality of their magnetism. Material habits attract material things and spiritual habits attract spiritual things. Bad habits attract bad things, good habits attract good things.

Peaceful thoughts and peaceful friends always produce healthy, magnetic minds.

To be firm is magnetic; to be just is magnetic; to be kind is magnetic.

Concentration develops great magnetism

To acquire mental magnetism, we must do everything with deep concentration. People who have reached the top in any profession or business have great magnetic power.

Every time you are looking, or listening, or lifting your hands, you are throwing out magnetic current. If you are absent-minded, you have no magnetism.

When you send a thought, you are sending energy with it. If you are thinking one thing while doing something else, then your energy is divided. When you are fully attentive to what you are doing, then you are developing magnetism.

WILL POWER CREATES MAGNETISM

The greater the will, the greater the flow of Life Energy.

Man's strong will, which refuses to be discouraged by anything and which flows continually and energetically toward the accomplishment of an object, becomes divinely empowered. The strong will of man is divine will.

How can you strengthen your will power? First, you must know the difference between "wish" and "will." "Wish" is a desire, but "will" means desire plus energy. If you did not use your will power, do you know what you would become? You would have to lie down and not move at all. Even if you were to move your hand, you would be using your will power.

The human will, when guided by error, is very bad, but when your will is tuned in with wisdom, it is guided by Divine Will.

Carrying a thought with dynamic will power means entertaining that thought until it assumes an outward form. When your will power develops that way, and when you can control your destiny by your will power, then you can do tremendous things.

Before you will to do a thing, reason about it. Make sure that you are directing your will toward accomplishing something good and helpful to yourself and others.

Everything that you see in this world is the result of will power, but it is not always used consciously. There is mechanical will and conscious will. Only by using your conscious will power rightly can you contact God's will, which is guided by wisdom. If you tune your will with wisdom, it is God's will by which you are being guided, but God's will often becomes buried beneath the conflicts of human life and we do not see His will for us.

You must never use blind will, and you must be sure that your will power is used constructively, not for harmful purposes or trifling things.

Always be sure that what you want is right for you to have, then use all the forces of your will power to accomplish your objective, all the time keeping your mind on God. No other desire must be in your heart but to know God; then all things will come to you.

To create dynamic will power, determine to do all the things in life that you thought you couldn't do, and devote your entire will power to accomplishing one thing at a time. Be sure that you have made a good selection, then refuse to submit to failure.

Use your will power to perfect yourself in this life. You must depend more and more upon the mind because mind is the creator of your body and your circumstances.

The effect of diet on your mind and magnetism

Our diet affects our disposition to a great extent. It affects our state of mind either favorably or unfavorably, and whatever affects our state of mind affects our disposition.

It is necessary to eat the proper food in order to make a proper brain as well as a proper body. All food has some relation to the mind.

The human machine is not unlike an automobile or a steam engine. The efficiency and general behavior of mechanical engines are largely dependent upon the fuel supplied to them; similarly, the condition of the human machine is largely dependent upon the food that a person eats.

Food has much to do with developing character, ability, social habits, and so forth.

The quality of a food's taste and color is reported to the brain through the nerves of taste and sight, and is experienced as a specific pleasant or unpleasant sensation. All these sensations are elaborated into perceptions and conceptions. Repeated conceptions about foods form definite mental habits, and manifest themselves as material, active, or spiritual qualities.

All foods have one of three qualities — some foods have spiritual qualities, some have activating qualities, and some have evil qualities.

Sattwic [uplifting] foods include fruits, vegetables, whole grains and legumes, honey, fresh dairy products, coconut milk, peanut and almond pastes, and nuts. These foods produce calmness and nobility.

Rajasic foods are those that produce active, worldly, strong, and emotional qualities of the mind. These foods include onions, garlic, eggs, horseradish, pumpkin, potatoes, pickles, and spices, as well as fish, fowl, and lamb.

Tamasic foods have darkening, destructive qualities. Foods that are full of odor, putrefied, or artificially made (deprived of their natural qualities) are tamasic. Examples are Roquefort cheese, cold storage foods, and liquors, as well as beef, veal, and pork. These foods produce pride, jealousy, greed, and vengefulness.

Animals, when killed, leave vibrations of fear, anger and suffering in their meat, which affect the mind of the consumer.

While we know that material foods supply the body with energy, we must also remember that good thoughts are nourishing food for the mind, and thoughts of any other nature are poisonous to the health of body and mind.

Since the expression of the soul is dependent upon the body, and the body is dependent upon food, it is desirable to know not only the physical, but also the spiritual and psychical effects of food.

Some spiritual qualities of food are:

Nuts: Help deep thinking, good for brain power and concentration.

Fruits: Develop heart and spiritual qualities.

Vegetables: Give power of management over the body.

Cereals: Produce strength of character.

Milk and Eggs: Give enthusiasm, fresh energy.

Spiritual qualities of some fruits are: peaches, selflessness; grapes, spiritual love; banana, humility; strawberry, dignity; pineapple, courage; cherries, cheerfulness.

All worry, care, and thought of difficulties should be put aside, particularly while eating and one should always partake of food with a thankful, joyful heart. The mind must take control and master the environment to see that there is only calmness and pleasantness at meal time if the digestive system is to function normally.

Food should not be eaten with the consciousness that it will produce physical health only, but rather that it will spiritualize the body.

Habits have to be recognized also. You must gradually change yourself. Remember, you must eat to live, not live to eat. Greed is a servant of the palate and is an enemy of digestion, good disposition, and general health. Greed wants to please the sense of taste at the cost of the happiness of the possessor of the sense of taste.

Eat to nourish the body, not for greed or to please the palate only. Think of your health and digestion and do not concentrate on your palate if you want to conquer greed.

Self-control, frugal eating, good mastication, plain food, eating only when you are very hungry, develop right habits of eating.

By eating too much solid food you lose your magnetism, and too much meat causes you to lose your magnetism because animal magnetism tampers with your spiritual magnetism.

It is found, by comparison of national characteristics of different nations, that our food is largely responsible for our mentalities. Too much meat produces a fighting quality; vegetables produce peace-loving qualities.

Every form of beef and pork should be strictly avoided. Those who feel that they must eat meat should confine themselves to lamb, chicken, and fish. It is better to eat eggs and nuts in place of meat, or use good meat substitutes.

Preserve the body temple for the Spirit to dwell in and deliver sermons of Truth and perfect health to all.

Affirmation

Today I will strive to be a spiritual magnet.

I will draw good to myself

according to my power of attraction.

Prayer-Demand Before Taking Food

Heavenly Father,

Receive this food. Make it holy.

Let no impurity of greed defile it.

The food comes from Thee.

It is to build Thy temple.

Spiritualize it.

Spirit to Spirit goes.

We are the petals of Thy manifestation,

but Thou art the flower,

its life, beauty, and loveliness.

Permeate our souls with the fragrance of Thy presence.

Chapter 2

BECOME MAGNETIC WITH RADIANT JOY

The magnetic power of a smile

Make your home a valley of smiles instead of a vale of tears.

Smile *now* and never mind how hard it has been for you to do so.

Smile *now*.

All the time remember to smile *now*, and you will smile *always*.

If you enjoyed good health for fifty years and then were sick for three years, unable to get healed by any method, you would probably forget about the length of time that you enjoyed good health and laughed at the idea of sickness. Now your reaction should be exactly the opposite. Just because you may have been sick for three years is no reason for thinking that you will never be well again.

Likewise, if you were happy a long time, and you have been unhappy a comparatively short time, you are apt to lose hope of ever being happy again. This is lack of imagination. The memory of a long-continued happiness should be a forceful subconscious habit to influence your conscious mind and ward off the consciousness of your present trouble.

You want a thing as long as you are not able to get it; when you have secured it, sooner or later you will tire of it, and then you will want something else. Have you ever tried to find that will-o'-the-wisp of "something else" which you seek at the end of all accomplished desires?

No matter what you seek, you must seek it *with* joy, in expectation of having joy by possessing it, and you must feel joyous when you actually get it. When seeking different things directly or indirectly, in reality you are seeking joy. When seeking all things, it is really joy that you seek through all these things and the fulfillment of all desires. Then, why not seek joy *directly*? Why seek it through the medium of material desires and material things? You do not want those things in life which bring you sorrow. Neither do you want those things which promise a little joy in the beginning but sink you in deep remorse and suffering in the end.

Why seek joy by supplicating the favor of short-lasting material things? Why depend upon short-lasting material things for short-lasting joys? Material things and fulfillment of material desires are short-lasting; therefore, all joys born of them are short-lasting. Joys born of eating, smelling fragrance, listening to music, beholding beautiful objects, and touching pleasing things are short-lasting. They last only as long as the sensations born of the senses of taste, smell, hearing, sight, and touch last.

You do not want a tantalizing joy; you do not want a transitory joy which brings sorrow in its trail; you crave joy which will not disappear like the sudden flicker of gossamer wings beneath the flash of lightning. You should look for joy which will shine forever steadily, like the ever luminous radium.

Neither do you want a joy which has too much sameness; you want a joy which changes and dances itself in many ways to enthrall your mind and keep your attention occupied and interested forever. Any joy that comes by fits and starts is tantalizing; any joy that is monotonous is, of course tiresome; any joy that only comes for a little while and brings sorrow at last is undesirable. Any joy that comes for a little while then flits away, sinking you in a state of indifference, and thus deepens that state by contrast, is torturing.

The joy that rhythmically changes all the time like the different poses of an actor, and yet remains unchangeable in itself, is what all of us are seeking. Such joy can only be found through regular, deep meditation. Such an ever-new, unchangeable fountain of joy alone can quench our joy-thirst.

If nature gave to us all at once everything we wanted — wealth, power, and lost friends — we would sooner or later get tired of all of these, but one thing we can never get tired of, and that is Joy itself. By its very nature, ever-new Joy is the only thing that can never tire the mind or make it want to exchange Joy for something else.

In the pursuit of evil or good, you are always seeking joy. The former promises joy and gives sorrow; the latter may promise sorrow but will surely give lasting joy in the end. Lasting, ever-new Joy is God, and when you have found Him, you have the eternally elusive will-o'-the wisp "something else" which you always seek at the end of all fulfilled desires. Finding this "something else," you will not seek any farther. Finding this ever-new joy, you will find everything in it that you ever sought.

Material objects which give joy remain outside of the mind; they only gain entry into the mind through imagination. Joy, from its very nature, is something born of the mind and lives closest in it. External, material objects can be destroyed, but this joy within can never be destroyed if one knows how to keep it and unless the possessor of joy changes his mind and becomes sorrowful. This joy is ever-new and indestructible.

Do not seek joy through material mediums, or desires born of such contact. Seek the unconditioned, indestructible Pure Joy within yourself, and you will then have found the ever-conscious, ever-new Joy-God. This joy is not an abstract quality of mind, but it is conscious, self-born, and is the conscious, self-expressing quality of Spirit. Seek it and be comforted forever.

When you have attained this ever-new joy, you will not have become a cynic, hating everybody. Rather, it is then that you will be in a position fit to enjoy everything rightly. As an immortal child of God, you are supposed to enjoy everything with a lasting attitude of your eternal nature of perpetual joy. People who enjoy material things become materially-minded. It is a disgrace to behave like a discontented mortal when you are made in God's image, and when you are immortal.

When immortals behave like mortals, they experience the changes of joy, sorrow, and indifference in their natures. That is why you must destroy this grafted nature of changeability on your unchangeable nature of joy. And when you have found your own nature of unchangeable joy, you will be able to enjoy everything, either pleasant or disagreeable with your unchangeable, indestructible joy. Your joy will stand unshaken amidst the crash of breaking earthly pleasures.

CONTENTMENT MAKES YOUR LIFE MAGNETIC

To be content does not mean passive resignation to evil, nor unnecessary and unproductive sufferings that might be cured, nor does it mean dumb submission to pain and injury, nor an expressionless existence.

❖ ❖ ❖

Contentment has in it an element of cheerful renunciation. It also includes a keen realization of the possession of things that are *really* worthwhile.

❖ ❖ ❖

We *attain* contentment; we are not born with it.

Contentment and satisfaction do not come with the possession of things; neither does prosperity consist in the possession of wealth. The possession of and the care for things can become a real burden. On the other hand, the relief in the realization that we are no longer responsible for material possessions is often very keen. The perception of one's powers and limitations is in itself a source of contentment.

A created want becomes a natural want in time through habit. Whatever the want may be, it gives pain. The more wants we have, the greater the possibilities of pain, for the more wants we have, the more difficult it is to fulfill them, and the more wants that remain unfilled, the greater is the pain.

If desire finds no prospect of immediate fulfillment, or finds an obstruction, then pain immediately arises. Why do we desire and long for things? Why do we yearn for states of mind, of feeling, of soul qualities and attainments? It is because we remember that once we were perfect, and it is for that long-lost perfection that we yearn. We are all children of God.

Purpose and aim are the qualities which make or mar an individual's life. If we have a driving purpose in life, we can tap the resources of the Infinite for power, and if that stirring purpose is in tune with the oneness of all Creation, we shall come to find life growing richer and wider. Such motives build the eternal things of Spirit, and they never fail.

If you fail while putting forth your best, your utmost cheerful effort, you have *not* failed. Get up and march on. You must be patient and persevering. Nothing is accomplished by those who are impatient or easily discouraged.

Magnetic happiness from the highest Source

You may have every legitimate wish fulfilled in this life and enjoy all your possessions, provided you have them and enjoy them with the consciousness of God. Supreme knowledge is within us. No outside agency can bring it to us or take it away from us.

We can begin to know God by first knowing ourselves, and as we grow in our knowledge of God, we will advance in knowledge of ourselves. It is the nature of God to express His perfection through man, but man's mind is so filled with the outer things of life that there is no time or place for the inner Real Self to come forth.

Since the attainment of health, success, and happiness by material methods is limited and uncertain, you must learn how to receive health and energy from Cosmic Energy, how to receive the power to create at will the things you need by learning the art of super-concentration, and how to receive happiness from the actual contact of the Supreme Inner Being and Force.

True happiness can come only from being in tune with the Infinite, just as lasting prosperity can come only by knowing the law governing prosperity. However, prosperity may be swept away in an instant, but no power can disturb your inner poise and knowledge once it has been attained. We gain strength by tuning our thoughts with the vibrations from God, until at last, like the wave that has become one with the ocean, we have become one with all Infinitude.

The yearning for our lost perfection, the urge to do and be the noblest, the most beautiful of which we are capable, is the creative impulse of every high achievement. We strive for perfection here because we long to be restored to our Oneness with God.

Since everyone's ultimate desire is to be happy and to have the joy of making others happy, and since God is the source of all happiness, there is no way you can avoid Him. And why should you? All else will betray you with lies and false promises; for naught but God can give you true and lasting joy.

In the beginning of life, in the middle of life, at the end of life, seek the happiness of God, because that alone will free you forever from all sorrows.

If you think money will give you happiness, you are wasting your time; it will never do so. If you are seeking human love, you will find in God a love that is a multi-million times greater.

To find God is to receive everything the heart craves. And whatever you think you need you will find fulfilled in God. To be spiritual is to open doors to health, happiness, and success. Therefore a study of the scientific conduct of

life is really important. To learn how to banish suffering
and attain the joy that cannot be taken away is something
practical. If I had not had this study from my childhood,
I would have made a horrible failure of my life.

By scientific meditation become a true devotee, that
like the moon you dispel the darkness around yourself
and others. Without realization through meditation, religion is the most mysterious book of all; you will never
be able to understand it. But by meditation you have the
proof of God's existence.

Go to your room and shut the door — make no fuss. Sit
down and talk to God. Practice meditation. Let your mind
become so intense that the next time you sit to meditate
you won't have to make the effort; your mind will be fixed
immediately on Him. If you don't make a great effort to
conquer physical and mental restlessness in the beginning, you will have difficulty every time you meditate
throughout the years. But if you make that supreme effort
at the start, you will soon be happy and free.

When I utter the name "God" my whole being melts away in His joy. But that I had to work for. Make the effort. I was not at first the devotional kind. My mind used to be very restless. But now it is just like fire. As soon as I put my mind at the Christ center between the eyebrows, all thoughts are gone — breath, heart, and mind are instantly still, and I am aware only of Spirit.

Make religion real by scientific methods. Science gives you definiteness and certainty. Sit quietly and practice the methods that have been given by great yogis of India: Mahavatar Babaji, Lahiri Mahasaya, Swami Sri Yukteswar.[*]

Find in yourself that supreme blessedness of which I speak to you, and when you do you will see that religion is no longer a myth but a scientific certainty. Pray to Him, "Lord, You are the Master of creation, so I come to You. I will never give up until You talk to me and make me realize Your presence. I will not live without You."

---

[*] The Masters of Kriya Yoga, described in Yogananda's *Autobiography of a Yogi.*

Affirmation

Having Thee as the deepest joy
of deepest meditation
I know that all things,
prosperity, health, and wisdom,
will be added unto me.

Chapter 3

OVERCOME THE OBSTACLES
TO MAGNETISM

OVERCOMING MATERIAL DESIRE TO INCREASE YOUR MAGNETISM

Material things cannot be owned by anyone, for at death they must be left behind and given to others. We are only allowed the *use* of things.

It is foolish to be attached to material things. You should only pray to be given the use of things which you *need*, to be given the power to create at will what you *need*. It is foolish to think that you are rich and then at death be compelled to give up everything, because even a millionaire must leave his wealth at the call of death.

Be like Jesus, who was rich with God in life, having nothing material, yet having all after death. In your earth life, to be a millionaire or a poor man is the same, if you but understand.

If you owned the earth, it would be nothing and would be fraught with sorrows, for at the time of death the delusion of its being wrested from you would torture your soul. To die of a broken heart and enter the grave with unfulfilled desires, while seeing or playing in this earthly movie house, is extremely foolish, for the picture house of this earth can never afford the perfect happiness of Spirit.

The only way to combat earthly disappointments of prosperity, fame, and happiness is not to feel sorry when you are denied what you think you should have.

Of course, you will say, "Our desires are conditioned by our needs." That is true, but I am speaking of the greater freedom of mind and soul: when you attain that, nothing can produce unhappiness because, having nothing, you can have all. When you possess the all-in-all God Consciousness, even though you have no material possessions, yet you have all.

The person who finds God owns the cosmos and, owning the cosmos, he owns everything in it. Jesus knew that he was one with the Father. That is why he could do things which many mortals could not do.

So, do not desire to be a millionaire. Instead, spend your time in daily meditation, longer and deeper, which is the quickest way to become Christ-like. To strive for God-contact in meditation is pure joy. You will be happy when you meditate, and you will be happier when you arrive at the end of the trail of meditation and meet God, the King of ever-new happiness.

When Jesus said, "Foxes have holes, and birds of the air have nests, but the son of man hath nowhere to lay his head," he was not bemoaning his poverty. Instead, he was saying that he was the owner of the cosmos, because he did not remain caged in a small place as earthly creatures do. Jesus also said, "Bread, the men of the world seek after (matter-loving, short-sighted persons), but seek ye first the Kingdom of God (the entire cosmos), and all these things (prosperity, wisdom, happiness) shall be added unto you (without your asking)."

This earth is a place of mirth, a pleasure house for immortals. Because we forget this and become identified with the earthly play, we suffer. We must remember that our real home is the mansion of changeless, ever-new, blissful, omnipresent immortality. We are eternally God's children, whether naughty or good, but when we forget that our home is God's kingdom and get mixed up with the earthly show, we make ourselves miserable. We must learn that we are immortal, made in God's blissful image.

There is one thing you will never tire of, either in this life or throughout eternity, and that is the ever-new joy realized in God-contact. Joy that is always the same may cause boredom, but joy that is ever-new will last forever. Such joy can be found only in deep meditation.

OVERCOMING REVENGE AND HATRED TO INCREASE YOUR MAGNETISM

Anger gives birth to jealousy, hatred, spite, vengeful-ness, destructiveness, "brain storms," temporary insanity leading to horrible crimes, and so forth. When anger attacks you, conquer it. When you are angry, say noth-ing. Knowing it to be a disease (like a cold, for instance), throw it off by a mental warm bath. Fill your mind, to the exclusion of all else, with thoughts of those with whom you can never be angry, no matter what they do.

When a desire of yours is obstructed, it usually results in anger. First, find out whether your desire was good or bad. If it was bad, you should be grateful to be released from wrongdoing.

Be calm; be firm.

When wrath comes, you forget your position; when you forget your position you do wrong things, thereby becoming a tool of ignorance. If something has gone wrong, correct the error. Look at things intelligently and peacefully. The divine law will give you the right understanding.

If you want to conquer any person, make him break his sword. Conquer evil with love: That is divine strength. It is much stronger than anger. The person who is angry with you should draw from you an ocean of love and of calmness, which will quench the fire of his wrath. Learn to give love, calmness, and continuous understanding to those who are angry.

Remember, when you are angry, you are in a slow baking oven. All your nerves, your brain cells, and flesh are baking in the fire of anger, which at times has caused even death. Anger carried to extremes is not safe for the body, mind, or soul. Many illnesses are caused by anger, which also distorts the face and brings on old age quickly.

Do not in this way desecrate your face and mind, which are made in the image of God.

Jesus showed how great he was when he said, "Father, forgive them, for they know not what they do." He showed that he was God. If he had, in anger, used all the powers at his command to destroy others, would mankind worship Him today? No! He showed his Godlike qualities and is now enshrined in every heart. He is the luminary that we behold throughout eternity: a light to warm us and to give us strength.

Try to conquer ugly, negative behavior by positive, good behavior. Always try to overcome inharmony by the display of the best that is in you. Self-reformation, self-control, positive behaviorism, control of speech, sweet words, and so on, are powers which make the soul clothed in robes of magnetism.

Love is the great antidote for anger. Do not be demonstrative in your love for an angry person. He is not in the mood to appreciate it, his reasoning faculty and good nature being temporarily paralyzed. All you can do is to give him your good will.

The expression of righteous indignation for the purpose of averting evil is, of course, productive of good.

If your anger is too violent, take a cold shower, douse the head with cold water, or put ice on the medulla and the temples just above the ears, on top of the head, and on the forehead, especially between the eyebrows.

Develop metaphysical reason and destroy anger. Look upon your anger-arousing agent as a child of God, a little five-year-old baby brother who unknowingly perhaps stabbed you. You must not feel a desire to stab this little brother in return. When you become Christ-like and look upon all humanity as little brothers hurting one another —"for they know not what they do"— then you cannot feel angry with anyone. Ignorance is the mother of all anger.

Mentally destroy anger; do not permit it to poison your peace and disturb your habitual joy-giving serenity.

When anger comes, think of love; think that, as you do not want others to be angry with you, so you do not wish others to feel your ugly anger.

When anger comes, start your machinery of calmness going; let your calmness move the cogwheel of peace, love, and forgiveness. With these antidotes, destroy anger.

It is a common blunder for people to try to conquer anger in others by anger, when anger can be conquered only by love.

To try to suppress evil people by fire and sword is ineffectual; even if their bodies are conquered by evil power, their souls remain stronger in evil and anger just the same. In order to conquer evil, one must use the divine power of love.

Millions of people are doing evil, but they are not dramatically punished by powerful forces sent from heaven, because God wants to conquer them only by love and wisdom whispered to them through their own conscience. Since God has given man free will to choose between good and evil, He therefore does not interfere with man by stopping his evil actions by use of heavenly powers.

God tries to influence his error-stricken children through the humble forgiving personalities of his true saints and devotees. Christlike souls who commune with God have distinctly declared that anyone who aspires to know Him must behave in a God-like manner and must learn to conquer evil by good, hate by love, revengeful actions by loving helpful actions, unkindness by kindness, harshness by sweetness, pride by humbleness, cruelty by kindness, unrighteousness by righteousness, falsehood by truth, jealousy by love, temptation by meditation, restlessness by calmness, harsh speech by sweet speech, evil behavior by good behavior, selfishness by unselfish behavior, theological arrogance by Self-realization.

Affirmation

I make up my mind never again
to wear anger on my face.
I will never inject the poison of anger
in the heart of my peace
and thus kill my spiritual life.

Prayer

O Spirit, Father,
save me from attacks of the fever of wrath,
which burn my brain, shock my nerves,
and poison my blood.

O Father, when I am angry,
place before me my mirror of introspection,
wherein I shall behold my face
made horrid and ugly by my wrath.
Father, I do not like to be seen with a disfigured face,
so do not let me make my appearance before others
with a wrath-wrecked countenance.

Father, teach me to dissolve this anger,
which makes me and others so unhappy and miserable.
Bless me, that I may never soil by selfish vexation
the love of those whom I love
and who love me.
Bless me, so that I shall not feed my anger
by allowing myself to become still more angry.

Teach me to cure anger-wounds
by the salve of self-respect and the balsam of kindness.
Command the lake of my kindness
ever to remain undisturbed
by the waves of misery-making anger-storms.

OVERCOMING REVENGE TO INCREASE YOUR MAGNETISM

Man is apt to be revengeful and unjust when he is judging the faults of others. We should treat the error-stricken as we would like to be treated if we ourselves were stricken with error. In the same spirit in which we judge others does the divine law judge us. Instead of judging with harshness, we should suggest with love.

Unkind, revengeful judging of the faults of others creates resentment and mental rebellion. A loving person does not cruelly judge and punish his brother, but he criticizes with love if necessary.

Prayer

Teach me not to increase their ignorance
by my wrong ways and revengefulness.
Teach me to make them better
by my forgiveness, self-control,
determination, wisdom, better example,
and prayer, and by Thy love.

Thou hast taught us not to increase
their delirious kicks of hatred by battering them
with the bludgeons of revenge.
Thine undying sympathy hath inspired us
to heal and wake our brothers,
suffering from the delirium of anger,
by the soothing salve of our forgiveness.

Affirmation

If I have any hatred,

revenge, or negation in my heart,

transmute it into Thy

all-forgiving love.

OVERCOMING AN INFERIORITY COMPLEX TO INCREASE YOUR MAGNETISM

An inferiority complex is born of contact with weak-minded people and the weak innate subconscious mind. A superiority complex results from false pride and an inflated ego. Both inferiority and superiority complexes are destructive to self-development. Both are fostered by imagination, ignoring facts, while neither belongs to the true, all-powerful nature of the soul.

Vikalpah means fanciful imagination. Fanciful imagination distorts all knowledge. It has nothing to answer to it in reality. To be touchy, to have an inferiority complex, to be sensitive: these come under "fanciful imagination."

Be proud only of the fact that you are a child of God! Correct your mortal attitude; take away the coverings of ignorance and find the light of Reality. Behold the Life that is behind all. Look within yourself.

You must realize that you are a child of God. Make up your mind that you are not going to be run by that old habit-bound self. The temporary limitations and imperfections of the body and brain cannot hold you back; as soon as you give the verdict and strongly will to be a new person, you will change.

Affirm that you are a child of God, and dwell on what Jesus said: "I and my Father are one."

As you develop spiritually you see that He is your true Self, reflected in you as the soul, just as the moon can be reflected in a vessel of water; you realize that you are the pure image of Divinity.

There must not be an inferiority complex any more than a superiority complex. What are you afraid of? You are neither a man nor a woman. You are not what you think you are; you are immortal, but not immortally identified with human habits, because they are your deadliest enemies.

An inferiority complex is just as bad as a superiority complex because if you have a superiority complex you are inferior, and if you are inferior, then you cannot be superior. So, remember that inherently you are truly the sons of God.

Essentially you are the children of God, so it is bad to think that you are inferior, and it is false to think that you are superior. When you try to bring in your own ego, you destroy God within you, so avoid having an inferiority or a superiority complex; they both retard the progress of the soul.

You must feel that God is with you, guiding you, and that God is your greatest love and your greatest superior. You are the servant of all, therefore you could not think of yourself as superior, and because God is with you, therefore you must avoid an inferiority complex or a superiority complex.

Resurrect your soul from the dreams of frailties. Resurrect your soul in eternal wisdom. What is the method? Relaxation, self-control, right diet, right fortitude, and an undaunted attitude of the mind. Do not acknowledge defeat.

Found your self-confidence upon actual achievements, and you will be free from all inferiority and superiority complexes.

Take long mental walks on the path of self-confidence. Exercise with the instruments of judgment, introspection, and initiative. Exhale poisonous thoughts of discouragement, discontentment, and hopelessness.

Always affirm your strength in God — *His* strength, through you.

To acknowledge defeat brings greater defeat. You have unlimited power; you must cultivate that power.

Meditation is the way to resurrect your soul from the bondage of the body and all your trials. Meditate at the feet of the Infinite. Learn to saturate yourself with God. Your trials may be great, but your greatest enemy is yourself. You are immortal; your trials are mortal. They are changeable, but you are unchangeable. You can unleash the eternal powers and shatter your trials.

Egotism is born of a superiority complex, whereas humbleness is born, not of an inferiority complex, but of wisdom.

Overcoming the obstacle of emotionalism to increase your magnetism

To maintain and develop an even mind without getting emotional is the way to magnetic living.

Emotionalism must be converted into power and be governed by wisdom; then one has great magnetism.

Technique for controlling emotions

Inhale and contract entire body all at once, gently.

Hold contraction counting 1 to 20, with deep attention upon the entire body.

Then exhale. Release contraction.

Repeat 3 times, or any time you feel weak and nervous.

OVERCOMING ANIMAL MAGNETISM

Animal organisms are held together by animal magnetism. The snake has great magnetic attracting power. It charms and draws little animals to itself by its animalistic magnetic power. Man, being a rational, moral, aesthetic, spiritual animal, possesses intellectual, moral, aesthetic, and spiritual magnetism, as well as animal magnetism. By animal magnetism, a man draws to himself physically-minded people. This animal magnetism is almost hypnotic in its effect.

Young people of opposite sexes, living on the material plane, often exchange their animal magnetism, blind one another by emotions and passions, and draw to themselves all kinds of destructive evil habits.

Hypnosis is a crime, since the hypnotizer robs his patient of free-will, judgment, and consciousness. Hypnosis practiced on an individual repeatedly for any length of time might affect the brain and make the mind mechanical, guided automatically by enslaving suggestions. Never allow yourself to be under the influence of anyone's animal magnetism or semi-hypnotic power. There is only a shade of difference between animal magnetism and hypnosis. When an individual exercises his animal magnetism on another person, the influenced one is constantly blinded and prejudiced by the wrong or right judgment of the stronger personality.

A person under the influence of animal magnetism may move here and there, yet be acting solely under the influence of another individual's instincts and habits. Here the consciousness is apparently free from the influence of hypnosis, but in reality is secretly guided and prejudiced by another person. Whereas an individual under the influence of hypnosis becomes unconscious of the surroundings and is aware only of the suggestions of the other individual. A hypnotized person is guided by his subconscious mind, and his conscious mind becomes almost entirely inactive. This is why no one should want to be influenced by animal magnetism or be hypnotized.

If one is a slave to any of the senses, he loses magnetism. If he has control over the senses, he develops magnetism.

CONTROLLING THE SEX FORCE CREATES STRONG INNER MAGNETISM

The sex force governed by wisdom can be used for the creation of a child on the physical plane, or for the creation of great thoughts on the mental plane, or for the development of the spiritual powers of self-control by absorption of sex force in the brain by divine meditation during the period of the appearance of sex consciousness in the body.

Anyone who practices physical exercises with deep concentration during a time of sex urge transmutes the sex energy into muscular energy. Those people who ignorantly concentrate on sex pleasure, not knowing how to transmute the sex energy for constructive purposes, only devitalize their body of energy, their mind of happiness, and their soul of divine bliss and wisdom.

Those unmarried people, who never break the law of celibacy, create in themselves a powerful magnetism which draws only their soul's companions, if they desire to marry.

Technique to transmute the sex energy

The best way to transmute sex impulses is to inhale and exhale deeply during sex excitement until the sex energy is transmuted into oxygen in the lungs. Then, during sex consciousness and during inhalation and exhalation, the mind should be kept busy affirming: "I want to transmute sex energy into spiritual energy. I want to turn it Godward to spiritually create."

Immediately after the sex impulse disappears by inhalation and exhalation, then read some holy Scripture or begin to meditate on the Spirit of the joy within.

Whenever the sex impulse revisits you, continuously inhale and exhale deeply. By inhalation and exhalation, tremendous energy is concentrated in the heart and lungs. Then the heart and lungs become magnets of living currents pulling away energy from all parts of the body, especially the sex region.

Then, when the brain becomes busy with deep God peace of meditation or some deep spiritual thought, the brain becomes a spiritual magnet pulling all the transmuted energy accumulated in the heart and lungs into the spiritual cerebral reservoir.

Affirmation

Since, through the law of attraction,
I have drawn unto me whatever conditions
I am now confronted with,
I will impersonally look my situation over,
and if I find things I do not like,
I shall change my thoughts,
and thus change the conditions.
Henceforth, I shall watch my thoughts
and be careful what kind of things I attract.

Chapter 4

INCREASE YOUR ABUNDANCE AND
SUCCESS MAGNETISM

Start by affirming success

Fill the cup of life today with thoughts of success! Cling no more to the memory of yesterday's failures, nor fret over clouds that might gather menacingly tomorrow.

I am made of God-substance,

since that is the only substance which exists.

Therefore I am health;

I am success;

I am peace.

I am youthful, I am youth,

I am healthy, I am health,

I am strong, I am strength,

I am joyful, I am joy,

I am successful, I am success,

I am peaceful, I am peace,

I am immortal, I am immortality.

Magnetize your efficiency and prosperity

What is real prosperity? You must find the real purpose of life; real prosperity lies in supplying the needs of the mental and spiritual as well as the physical man.

Knowledge of how to become prosperous is always important. Real prosperity comes by increasing the power of your mental efficiency by which you can supply the things you need. There is a great difference between things that you *need* and things that you *want*.

If you know how to withdraw your attention from all objects of distraction and place it upon one object of concentration, then you know how to attract at will what you need. When you find the answers to everything within yourself, then you can say, "I am prosperous."

Real prosperity means when you have all things at your command — the things that are necessary for your entire existence. But very few people understand in what lies real necessity. Very few people know the real meaning of "needs." If the need is boiled down to certain definite things, then the need can be easily satisfied.

Money is not a curse. It is the manner in which you use money that is important. You ask a dollar bill, "Shall I buy poison with you?" It doesn't answer, but if you misuse this brainless dollar, it will punish you. When you use it rightly, it gives you happiness. There is no saint who does not use money in his work. Whoever eats has to pay for the food, and it is better to be able to buy your food than to live on charity.

Most people spend all their mental energy trying to make money, and some who are successful die of heart failure before they are able to secure happiness. If you have lots of health and lots of wealth and lots of trouble with everybody and yourself, you have very little. The entire purpose of life becomes futile when you cannot find true happiness.

When wealth is lost, you have lost a *little*.

When your health is lost, you have lost *something*.

But when your peace is lost, *all* is lost.

Most people develop mental efficiency as the by-product of their efforts for material success. Few people know that money is made for happiness, but happiness cannot be found just by developing desire for money. Mental efficiency depends upon the art of concentration. You must know the scientific method of concentration by which you can disengage your attention from objects of distraction and focus it upon one thing at a time without deviation.

By visualizing efficiency, or by affirmations, you may strengthen your subconscious mind, which in turn encourages your conscious mind, but that is all that visualization or affirmation alone can do.

The conscious mind still has to achieve the success and is hindered by the law of cause and effect.

The conscious mind cannot initiate a new cause which will bring positive success in any direction, but when the human mind can contact God, then the superconscious mind can be sure of success, due to the unlimited power of God and due to creating a new cause of success.

TURN FAILURE INTO SUCCESS

Whatever your position in life, it is you who put yourself there. Whatever you have made yourself in the past, that is what you are now.

God never punishes or rewards you, for He has given you the power to punish or reward yourself by the use or misuse of your own reason and will. It is you who transgressed the laws of health, prosperity, and wisdom and punished yourself with sickness, poverty, and ignorance.

One cause of failure is that you do not weigh your bad habits against the power of your free will required to combat them. Most people fail in attaining their material, mental, and spiritual desires because of the lack of definite purpose and sustained effort.

Extraordinary talent is not as necessary as unswerving purpose and unfailing application and effort. Do not continue to carry your burden of old mental and moral weaknesses acquired in past years, but burn them in the fires of resolution and become free.

Remember that the right method of meditation is the only lasting way to all-round freedom and success. You must consciously contact God, and finding Him first, you will have attained dominion over yourself and over all your limiting conditions.

EXCHANGING MAGNETISM

We must be careful with whom we associate, because we are continually exchanging magnetism with other people through our thoughts, through shaking hands and through looking into the eyes of another person.

As soon as we shake hands with someone, a magnet is formed. The person who is the stronger gives his vibration to the other person.

People should first decide what kind of magnetism they want and then choose the particular persons who possess it.

For instance, if you are a failure and you want success, associate and shake hands as much as possible with those who have attained success in their business, art, or profession.

Of course, it is not always easy to make such contacts, but "where there's a will, there's a way."

A spiritual man, but a material failure, attentively shaking hands with a spiritually weak but more prosperous business man would make two magnets. Through the two pairs of feet, forming the two poles of a magnet, would be exchanged physical qualities, and through the two hands, forming the two poles of another magnet, the mental qualities will be exchanged.

If such hand-shaking and mental contacts with deep attention is kept up, then the business man would be more spiritual, and the spiritual man would be more materially prosperous through the virtue of the upper magnet. There would be also exchange of their bad qualities through the power of the lower magnet in the pact. The spiritual man and the business man both might be affected in their vocational qualities.

We will now take a different case, that of an idealist of weak character who endeavors to influence a stubborn, confirmed evil-doer. By close association and oft-repeated handshaking, it is quite likely that the reformer will become a positive pole, drawing evil qualities, and the evil-doer will become a negative pole, passively drawing good qualities in a very limited way. In this case, the idealist would end up being the one who is negatively changed. Therefore, unless one has grown very strong spiritually, he should not attempt to reform the very wicked.

When shaking hands, the magnetism is naturally exchanged. Positive-negative combinations form themselves into inner magnets.

In developing and exchanging magnetism between two persons, the stronger magnetism will predominate. If both are equally strong, each will be absorbed to some extent by the other, resulting in good to each, if the qualities are good. If one is good and one is evil, either has a chance of predominating.

After deep meditation, affirm: "Father, send to me my proper business associate through my spiritual magnetism increased through Thy Grace."

The importance of environment

Environment is of supreme importance. It is greater than will power. You must surround yourself with good environment.

We become like the people we mingle with, not through their conversation, but through the silent magnetic vibration which goes out of their bodies. When we come in the range of their magnetism, we become like them.

If a man wants to become an artist, he must associate with artists. If he wants to be a good business man, he must associate with successful leaders. If he wants to become a spiritual giant, he must associate with devotees of God.

If a weak man wrestles or lives in the same room with a strong, vital individual, he absorbs some of the latter's vital and mental magnetism. For this reason, young and old people should mingle and thus exchange magnetism. Different people have different kinds of vitality. Always try to discover new methods for getting direct energy qualities from different individuals.

The stronger magnetism wins

One weak negatively-evil individual plus one strong positively-good individual equals this: The positive-good magnetism will be predominant.

A great moral power plus a weak moral power equals a great moral magnetism.

A person of great positive anger plus a person of negatively mild disposition equals this: The positive-anger magnetism will reign.

A very strong, calm disposition plus a negative, slightly angry disposition, equals this: Magnetism of calmness will be predominant.

A strong, positive failure plus a lesser positive failure equals reinforced failure-magnetism.

A strong positive success plus a lesser positive success equals reinforced success.

A strong failure plus a strong success may equal either a strong failure magnetism, or a strong success magnetism, depending upon surrounding circumstances.

A great spiritual power plus a great business man equals a great spiritual magnetism and a great business magnetism.

A weak spiritual man and a great evil power equals a great evil magnetism. A great spiritual power plus a weak evil power equals a great spiritual magnetism.

Great intellectual power plus great ignorance may equal either great intellect or great ignorance. A great intellect plus a small intellect equals a great intellect.

Gain success through spiritual principles

God is the secret of all mental power, peace, and prosperity. Then why use the limited, impossible human method of gaining prosperity? By visualizing abundance, or by affirmation, you may strengthen your subconscious mind, which may in turn encourage your conscious mind, but that is all that visualization alone can do. The conscious mind still has to achieve the success just the same and is hindered by the working of the law of cause and effect. The conscious mind cannot initiate a new cause which will bring positive success in any direction, but when the human mind can contact God, then the superconscious mind can be sure of success due to the unlimited power of God and due to creating a new cause of success.

After establishing that the goal of life is maximum efficiency, peace, health, and success, let us consider the surest way to prosperity. Prosperity does not consist just in the making of money; it also consists in acquiring the mental efficiency by which man can uniformly acquire health, wealth, wisdom, and peace at will.

The goal of your material life should be maximum business efficiency, peace, health, and general success. Material prosperity consists in acquiring the mental efficiency by which you can gain all these things at will. Great wealth does not necessarily bring health, peace, or efficiency, but acquirements of efficiency and peace are sure to bring balanced material success.

Man often forgets to concentrate on his little physical needs and on his great need of developing mental efficiency in everything and of acquiring divine contentment. Man is so busy multiplying his conditions of physical comfort that he considers very many unnecessary things as a necessary part of his existence.

Many persons have dived in the Ocean of Thy Abundance again and again to seek the pearls of opulence, power, and wisdom, but only a few divers have found them. These few persons have praised the wondrous riches of Thy Sea because they dived well and found the secret treasure nook. Those who dived in the wrong places blamed Thy blue brine of abundance as devoid of the most desired treasures. Many persons perish diving in the Sea of Treasures, being devoured by monsters of selfishness, greed, faithlessness, doubt, idleness, and skepticism.

Repeat this prayer daily

"Heavenly Father, teach me how to dive in Thy *Ocean of Plenty* again and again. If I do not find the pearls of Thy Perception by one or two divings, I will not say that Thy *Ocean of Everything* is empty, for Thou wilt show me that the fault is with my diving. I will put on the diving apparel of faith, power, and fortitude, and Thou wilt direct my mind to dive in the right place, where Thy bounty is hidden."

Affirmation

I am brave, I am strong.
Perfume of success thought
Blows in me, blows in me.
I am cool, I am calm
I am sweet, I am kind
I am love, I am sympathy
I am charming and magnetic.

Chapter 5

FAITH, HOPE, AND LOVE MAKE
YOU MAGNETIC

Cultivate faith in your life

No hope is too grand or too impossible for the all-seeing eye of intuitive faith, or ultimate perception through which we know all things as they are, to bring into manifestation. That is why in ordinary mortals we see the manifestation of Hope. When hope is used properly to work for the acquisition of the soul's lost intuition, then faith, or intuitive Self-realization, develops.

Faith gives birth to the human hope and the desire to achieve, but it also hides behind the wall of ignorance. Ordinary human beings know practically nothing of this intuitive faith latent in the soul, which is the secret spring of all our wildest hopes.

The word "faith" is often erroneously used for "belief," as, "I have faith in him." Belief is problematic and may be followed by disillusionment. Belief is the initial experimental feeling about the truth of anything. Untested belief crystallizes into dogmatic sentiment or, if discouraged, it may change into skepticism or unbelief.

When belief turns into dogmatic sentiment or skepticism, it is destructive. Constructive belief is the attitude of mind necessary for testing the truth about a thing in the beginning. The person who refuses to believe in anything, refuses to test and experiment. These are the only means by which to know Truth.

Constructive belief is good when one continuously believes and experiments with a truth until its real nature is revealed. Destructive disbelief is limiting because one disbelieves for the fun of doing so. Constructive disbelief or doubt is good because one assumes an attitude, not of final skepticism and turning forever away from Truth, but because one says, "Well, I am from Missouri; I shall not believe your statement until you prove that it is true."

According to Jesus, faith is the proof of things unseen; that is, all phenomena or visible matter can be recorded by the senses, but not invisible substances, such as vibrations, subtle Cosmic forces, and super-electric lights, which are unseen or unknown to, and unregistered by, the limited power of the senses.

The proof of the existence of all subtle forces and of God as final substance lies in faith, or the instantaneous all-knowing, all-seeing, intuitive power developed through deep meditation and soul contact.

Jesus said, "For verily I say unto you, if ye have faith as a grain of mustard seed, ye shall say unto this mountain, remove hence to yonder place, and it shall remove; and nothing shall be impossible unto you."— Matt. 17:20

If a fanatic, or mad man, or religious zealot strongly believes that he can move a mountain into the sea, and for years tries to do so, he can never accomplish the feat. Also, if a man says, in a meek, squeaky voice, "Mr.

Mountain, please go into the depth of the sea, for Jesus said it was possible to make you move, although I myself don't believe it," the mountain will not listen to that either. If, however, one has faith in, or intuitive knowledge of, Cosmic Consciousness as the prime mover of all atomic Creation, then, through that all-pervading consciousness one can act on or control any portion of matter on the earth or on a distant star.

Just as your consciousness is omnipresent in every part of your body, and as you can swing an arm or move your muscles, that is, you can cause consciousness to act in any part of the body, so the man of cosmic faith, or cosmic omnipresent consciousness, can cause any portion of matter to react to his command. This faith is inner light, in which the presence of all finer forces invisible to the eye and the senses are revealed as true.

Cultivate magnetic hope in your heart

People hope blindly or consciously due to the latent Divine Mason within, which intuitively reminds them that "All is not lost forever." Death and failure are not the final experience, for behind the dark clouds of temporary disillusionment awaits the silver lining of eternal fulfillment. We must keep hoping to know God even to the last breath, for we have all Eternity in which to hope for the best and the highest. The greatest insult to the soul is to label it with the consciousness of final despondency.

Hope is the eternal light on the dark pathway through which the soul must travel through incarnations in order to reach God. Never extinguish hope, as you would have to wait miserably on the pathway of darkness until you chose to rekindle your searchlight of hope and start again on your journey toward God.

Human beings hope and try for a while; but if they fail a dozen times, they cease to hope and become despondent. The divine man never ceases to hope, for he knows that he has all Eternity in which to materialize his dreams.

We must not think of death as an eternal abyss of oblivious sleep where we remain forever; but we must consider it as a caravansary where we rest for a while, so that we may with fresh hope and energy journey on and on until we reach our mansion of eternal fulfillment in God.

To kill hope and to be despondent is to put on an animal mask of limitation and to hide your Divine identity of Almightiness. Instead, hope for the highest and the best, for, as a child of God, nothing is too good for you. Keep on hoping. Move in that light until you travel through pathways of incarnations to your luminous home in God. Hope is born out of the intuitive consciousness in the soul that sometime or other we shall remember our forgotten image of God within us. This intuitive consciousness is faith.

Love

To have friends, you must manifest friendliness. If you open the door to the magnetic power of friendship, a soul or souls of like vibrations will be attracted to you.

To attract friends you must possess the qualities of a real friend.

Ugliness of disposition and selfishness drive away all friends of former incarnations, whereas friendliness draws them toward you. Therefore, be ready always to meet them half way. Never mind if one or two friends prove false and deceive you.

There are people who give you the instantaneous feeling that you have always known them. Often they are very near you, drawn by the friendship born in the dim, distant past. They constitute your shining collection of soul jewels.

Friendship is the universal spiritual attraction that unites souls in the bond of divine love and may manifest itself either in two or in many persons.

Practice kindness at home, and you will win everybody else by your magnetic aura of kindness.

The sun and moon and earth and all things are held together by the bonding force of God's love. If we want to know Him, we must not keep our love isolated and small, but conjoin it to divine love.

Through all the dance of life and death, know that God is love. The only purpose of life should be to find that love. There is no greater tonic. It can beautify man in both body and mind.

Love cannot be described or defined: It can only be experienced, as a deep feeling.

All love, in its native purity, is God's love.

If pure love shines in your soul, you will be clothed with God's ever-attracting, universal beauty and infinite love.

All nations should come together in the temple of universal love and understanding.

Love alone will last.

The laws of God are the laws of brotherhood and love.

Although man's love is born in his human relations and in recognition of mutual usefulness, yet pure love, as it evolves spiritually, transcends all outer relationships and becomes freed from every condition of mutual usefulness. Although love is born in that sense of usefulness, one ceases to be aware of any such outward condition. A mother's love for her child may be taken as an example, for it is unconditional. A mother may love even a wicked child.

Our love must not be limited to those who are near to us. The divine purpose of close relationships is to expand that love. Nature breaks the ties of family life only to teach us that the love we give our family needs to be extended also to our neighbors, our friends, our country, and to all nations.

One who does not love his family cannot love his neighbor or his country. One who does not first love his country cannot learn to love all countries.

Love is a condition of the mind and heart which essentially transcends all relationships. We should worship God above all through all these relationships. God can be loved as Father, Mother, Master, Friend, or the Divine Beloved of all hearts.

Love must never remain circumscribed in littleness. Through the gates of friendship, conjugal affection, parental love, and the love of one's fellow beings and of all animate creatures, we can enter into the kingdom of Divine Love. Pure love does not come by talking, but by culturing it gradually in the soil of an ever-increasing, ever-expanding feeling of sympathy and friendship toward all existence.

That person who has never loved anyone in particular can never love all humanity. One who has never loved his fellow beings, and even birds and animals, can never love God. Only in the soil of the heart where human love grows can divine love grow.

Magnetizing a united world

The wall of creed and the blinding greed for gold has divided human hearts. They live behind these self-erected prison walls of dogma and have lost sight of the Altar of Oneness on which Thy Temple of omnipresence is built.

Let us pulverize these walls of money, name, power, and dogma so that we may view the floor of Thy Universal Temple of Oneness and gather together there to offer unto Thee the chorus of our united love and the hymns of our hearts.

Let us call all Christian, Buddhist, Jewish, Mohammedan, and Hindu Temples by the one name — "Altar of God," or "Sanctuary of Our One Father."

Let us call the different teachings by one name — "Sermons of Wisdom."

Let us call all different races, the brown, the yellow, the red, and the white, by one name — "Human Brothers," children of our Father-Mother-God.

Let us call all countries — "United States of the World."

Let us call our government — "International Government of Truth."

Let us all train the soldiers of our hearts — love, faith, kindness, and understanding, and declare a world war against selfishness, church bigotry, industrial and individual greed, unkindness, territorial aggression, race and class prejudice, armaments, international distrust, poverty, sickness, spiritual ignorance, and blind, excluding patriotism.

Let us have the world policed by the guardian angel of true brotherhood, and let us have spiritual education of our hearts.

Let us live simply outside, but let us be supremely happy within.

Let us learn to build mansions of wisdom in the unfading garden of peace, which blooms with the million-hued blossoms of beautiful soul qualities.

Let us learn to use the aerial planes of imagination and intuitive vision to take flight in His Kingdom of Infinite Beauty and Bliss.

Let us soar in the Ark of Silence over the peaks of the highest wisdom, and let us roam in the land of endless beauty.

Let us get richer by acquiring the great wealth of peace, and become peace-millionaires.

Let us raise our own paradise, which lies buried in our fancy and let us bring the Living God of Pure Joy onto the altar of our hearts and worship Him there with the flowers of immortality and deathless devotion.

Affirmation

As I radiate love and good will to others,

I open the channel for God's love to come to me,

for Divine Love is the magnet

that will draw all good unto me.

Chapter 6

MAGNETIZE YOUR SOUL

If we use all our magnetism to gain material things, sooner or later we shall be disillusioned. It is true that God gave us bodies, and we must look after them; but if we first develop spiritual magnetism, it will guide us in the proper ways to supply all our material needs.

One can develop cosmic magnetism by thinking of God and saintly people. By concentrating deeply upon a certain personality, one can attract that personality. That is why one should think only of great individuals. If we concentrate on thoughts of wicked people, we will attract their qualities unless we are stronger than they are. If our whole heart is with someone, we draw all the defects and all the good qualities of that person.

If one is a material magnet, he notices that power in others he meets. If he is a moral magnet, he notices that power in others. If he is a spiritual magnet, he notices that magnetism in others.

Divine magnetism is the power of all powers. When our prayer bursts out of our heart and God gives up His vow of silence and speaks to us, then we have gained divine magnetism.

We must use our time to develop spiritual magnetism in order to attract the Imperishable. Develop power to attract the highest thing — then we can easily attract all lesser things.

We must detach ourselves from this body — this physical residence. Each of us is a spark of the Infinite. We must differentiate between perishable objects and imperishable possessions. Anything that belongs to the body is perishable; anything that belongs to the mind is semi-perishable; anything that belongs to the soul is imperishable.

Each individual life is the scene of a tug-of-war between God's indrawing magnetism and Satan's outwardly repulsing magnetism. Man's mind and senses are attracted to finite matter; his discrimination and intuitions are attracted to soul-pleasing actions and Spirit.

The soul, by the power of discrimination and intuition, tries to pull to itself, and to harmonious actions, all unifying noble bodily and mental forces. The satanic force wants the body projected and kept away from the influence of Divine magnetism, grovelling in finitude and inharmony.

The soul's power of moving toward God is called "soul magnetism." Soul magnetism consists in drawing to itself all good-reminding human experiences. Soul magnetism is the power by which an individual draws to himself friends, real desired objects, and the acquirement of the power to know everything about everything. It is God's magnetic drawing power, which is distributed and seated in every heart — in everything.

Man, being a rational, aesthetic, spiritual animal, possesses intellectual, moral, aesthetic, and spiritual as well as animal magnetism. The right kind of magnetic power has expanding, uplifting, and spiritual qualities. Some people are so magnetic that they inspire us and expand our consciousness. This is a sort of magnetic power that we all want, not the stupefying kind of hypnotic or animal magnetism.

Magnetism is a drawing, uplifting, expanding power. Magnetic power is a quality of the Spirit. We hear someone say: "Oh, I met a friend who is so magnetic that he inspired me, and expanded my consciousness."

One who contacts the Spirit's own magnetism by meditating upon OM and God, intuitively perceives all-attracting Divine Magnetism, and develops spiritual magnetism of limitless range.

The secret of habit and of magnetism is found in the scriptural verse, "For unto everyone that hath shall be given, and he shall have abundance; but from him that hath not shall be taken away even that which he hath." — Matt. 25:29

If you keep yourself morning, noon, and night dreaming, feeling, and sensing the all-attracting Divine Magnetism, your power can draw objects of desire from a distance and can uplift people by the mere contact of sight, or even by your simple wish or your powerfully directed uplifting concentration. By this power you can draw friends from afar — those who were real friends in a past life. By this power you can make the elements bow to your wish.

By the invitation of the Divine Magnetism, you can draw angels, all creative luminous forces, savants, and past saints to come to you and dance in your joy. By this Divine Magnetism you can draw to yourself all rays of knowledge, to come and sparkle and scintillate around your being.

Try to be humble instead of egotistical, and through the magnetism of humbleness attract the protecting presence of friends, saints, and God.

The humble person knows that there can be nothing greater than God, and therefore he draws God to himself through the fragrance of his humbleness.

Every mother should teach her marriagable daughter to emanate sincere smiles, and wear the rouge of sincerity and true love on her face. Every mother should teach her daughter to attract by spiritual magnetism only, and be fully dressed with all the real magnetic qualities of wisdom, understanding, thoughtfulness, consideration, presence of mind, true learning, and all-round efficiency. Spiritual magnetism will draw spiritual souls.

While we cannot force salvation upon others, we can do our best to set an example of well-being and bodily health, being a magnet which draws others' eyes toward us, to inspire them more.

INCREASE YOUR DIVINE MAGNETISM

God, being the Maker of everything, has power over your life, and as such your duty to Him is more important than your duty to the dream world which you are beholding. The ocean is made of waves. Each wave is made of drops of water. Take away the drops, and there is no ocean. So it is that God is made of us.

Everyone will find God in the end, but there are those who will delay. When you pull down the shades of the mind, God's sunlight cannot flow in, but when your mind is open, light can flow through it.

Most people live almost mechanically, unconscious of any ideal or plan of life. They struggle for a living, then leave the shores of mortality without knowing why they came here and what their duties were.

Swami Shankara, reorganizer of the Swami Order in India, who lived in the eighth century, and who was the greatest commentator on *Vedanta* philosophy, said, "The child is busy with play, youth is busy with sex, and old age is busy with worries. Few seek the salvation of the Spirit."

If you analyze yourself every day, you will notice how little you pray or meditate. Also notice that your mind will wander unless you are intense in your meditation and think of God all the time. If you spend the two hours in meditation that you usually spend in small talk, you will see how your life will change for the better.

The growth of a plant requires two things — the ground and the seed. In meditation, the seed is the mental preparation. If, in the back part of your mind you say, "I know I never shall contact God," you never will; but if you say with devotion, "Father, Father, Father," your soul, like a plummet which drops straight down, will straightway reach the depth of the sea.

When you become united with God, all your faults will leave you. Meditation is the only thing that will really change you. The only way to destroy weakness is to contact God. Then you will feel that the whole universe is yours; you will feel your presence in everything. You will be as conscious of this as you are conscious of your body. When you make up your mind that the only thing you want is God and pursue that idea with determination, then you will find Him.

Deep meditation keeps the consciousness always on God, and lack of meditation keeps the consciousness on the senses.

If you are not meditating and you still feel a nearness to God with you all the time you are working, you are retaining the full benefit of your recent meditation. If you can retain the joy and thrill of meditation during the entire day, you are still meditating. You are then unattached to the senses. When you can feel God in the flesh as well as in meditation, it is complete. That is what devotees who follow the path of meditation experience. They become detached; they do everything as a part of their duty but are not attached to it.

Occasionally, a soul realizes the joy that is in meditation and searches for God day and night; and although God doesn't answer, still he goes on until suddenly he finds God. We have to work to reach the Infinite, and work in the right way. No one can give you Self-Realization. You have to work for that reward. All the spiritual teachers in the world cannot give you salvation unless you make the effort to receive it.

Joy and God are One. Joy is the healing that you want first, the healing of the ignorance of the soul.

You will finally have to dump the physical body in the dust, so you must think of Spirit.

Affirmations are better than the usual form of prayers. Do not beg a favor from God. He will not break any law of His universe because you ask Him to, but when you demand your birthright as a child of His, then He will listen. A long prayer with words, words, words, does not mean anything at all, for then the mind is wandering. In an affirmation, one should both say and feel deeply the meaning of the thought behind the words; then the thought will go deeply into the conscious mind, then into the subconscious, and then into the superconscious; — when it registers in the superconsciousness it demonstrates.

Always affirm with intelligence and devotion until your thought goes consciously through the subconscious mind into the superconscious mind. The greatest healing you should pray for is the healing of your ignorance, so that you will never go back to the old form of life. The best and highest reward in our life toward God Consciousness is the realization of unceasing happiness, which we call Peace, or Bliss.

Before meditation, offer the following prayer:
"Beloved of the universe, be with us evermore.
Make us realize that Thou art the only king
sitting on the throne of all our ambitions.
Bless us, that we be not deluded into thinking
that other things are more important than finding Thee.

Thou are the only goal beyond the portals of life and
   death.

Thou art the End, where all incarnations shall commingle
in Thy presence.

Bless us, that we see only what is good,

hear only what is good,

smell, taste, and touch only what is good,

and think and will only what is good.

Day and night we will think of Thee and will reinforce
   our consciousness

while we meditate on Thee alone.

May Thy love shine forever on the sanctuary of our
   devotion,

and may we be able to awaken Thy love in all hearts.

Bless us, and be with us evermore."

Healing others with a strong magnetism

Wherever you go, scatter kindness; let your heart be charged with God, your feet charged with God, your eyes charged with God. That is what Jesus meant by the "laying on of hands," and that is what He meant when He said: "Be ye fishers of men."

All the parts of the body which come in pairs — eyes, ears, big and little tongues, hands, feet, and so on, receive and radiate positive and negative currents, and each pair forms a magnet with more or less power.

The optical magnet can charm, enthrall, and draw people so strongly that they may feel the magnetism of one's soul through the eyes.

Some highly-developed people are able to spiritualize or heal a whole audience just by the magnetism of the eyes.

The laying of the hands on sick people is done to send the healing x-rays of the hands into the body of the patient to electrocute the disease germs.

There is no power greater than the life force flowing

through the hands, provided it is made strong by an
indomitable will.

Affirmation

Whether soaring through the sky

encased in a steel air-cage,

or drawn o'er the land by snorting iron steeds,

or moving easily over smooth highways on rubber wheels,

or having my very thoughts paralyzed

by the pounding din of assembly lines,

the compass needle of my attention

will ever keep turning toward

Thy magnetic North Pole of divine love.

Chapter 7

THE MAGNETISM OF SPIRITUAL LIVING

Every noble thought that you have — it is God think-
ing through you. Why not receive magnetism from God?
Matter came, not to repress God, but to express God.
Realize this.

Sing with joy in God. So magnetize with your joy all
those who hear you sing that, eventually, the entire pro-
cession becomes a parade of souls singing joyfully to God.

We are soldiers of God who have come with the power
of love, the power of wisdom, and the power of spirituality to spread the fire of Spirit that burns all darkness
from lives.

You must not only get magnetism from people and
places, but you must get the magnetism which comes
from within through deep concentration and by going
beyond in the portals of meditation. Beyond the land

of peace, beyond the land of dreams, beyond the land of silence lies the garden of Self-realization.

Look to God and you shall be clothed with His magnetism.

This is the way to greater freedom. Concentrate upon changelessness and do not be affected by changes going on around you. Hold your center of peace and happiness. You become magnetized with God when your attention is upon God.

As the sun holds the planets and stars around it by its great magnetic force, so our ego binds our thoughts and cells together. If this ego is dead or unconscious, all the thoughts will gradually vanish from the body, the strings of forces will be burst asunder, and the cells will begin to decay.

The magnetism of meditation

Meditating together increases the degree of Self-realization of each member of the group, by the law of invisible vibratory exchange of spiritual magnetism.

God cannot be known by ignorant faith but by wise faith and continuous meditation. Any Christian mystic like St. Francis, who has known God, has spent hours in meditation and the practice of Christianity. It requires more than simple faith to know God. He must be experienced within. And no minister has a right to preach about God if he has not communed with Him. Did not Jesus say, "The blind cannot lead the blind"?

Jesus taught to the masses simple faith, for it is better to believe in God than in material life, but to His disciples he gave strict discipline and taught them to pray unceasingly. That means to pray until all disturbing thoughts leave the mind and the thought of God alone becomes uppermost there. Jesus taught his students to love God with all their hearts, which means that one should love God with the same great devotion that he feels for his family or dearest friend.

Jesus went further and taught his disciples to love God with all their mind, which means to love God with full concentration upon Him alone when praying to Him and not just idly saying the Lord's prayer while thinking about lesser things in the background of the mind. When Jesus said, "Love God with all your strength," he meant that one should withdraw the mind and energy from the body and place them on God. This we do in sleep unconsciously. The mind is no longer conscious of the body, and the energy is switched off from the five senses so that sensations of light, smell, taste, sight, or touch are not perceived.

When one does this consciously, he is able to place complete concentration upon God. By following the techniques of Self-realization you will learn in time, but not all at once, to switch off the current from the telephones of sight, hearing, smell, taste, and touch and unite it with God. This is what is meant by loving God with all one's strength. The disciples of Jesus knew of these methods, but the modern Christian world knows nothing of it.

Lastly, Jesus said, "Love God with all your soul." When one concentrates and gradually passes the psychic state, he reaches the superconscious state which lies beyond the state of deep sleep. Here he learns to develop his intuitive powers and feels the soul as the perfect image of God. This final state requires years of study and meditation and prayer. Only when the soul is known does one really know God. That is why the ancients said, "Know Thyself." The true Self is the soul, which is the image of God within every individual.

Last of all, please remember that as you cannot satisfy hunger by feeding someone else, or as you cannot reach the top of one of the high buildings in Chicago by merely thinking you are there, so you cannot reach God by imagination.

The master minds of India sent Self-realization teachings here because Jesus Christ, who communed with them, was grieved that the Christian world has made Christianity only a social uplifting religion and has forgotten the method of directly communing with God.

TAKE CARE OF YOUR SPIRITUAL GROWTH

The most direct path toward spiritual growth is to practice the scientific methods that have been taught by the great yogis of India. These scientific methods will give you definiteness and certainty.

Science systematizes everything into a definite conception. You must make religion scientific. Combine two things in a certain way and you will get a certain result. The Masters of India are telling you why you should seek God and telling you how to find Him. You must make the laws of God a practical part of your life. In India we are taught to make spirituality practical. We want to know God. We take religion seriously.

Science and religion should go hand in hand. All the results of science are definite and connected by reason. When Jesus urged His disciples to have faith, He didn't mean just blind faith.

The yoga teaching is definite and scientific. Yoga means "scientific unity of soul and God." It does away with all dogma. The spiritual Masters in India never tell their disciples they will find God in a minute. We must work hard to find Him. We must make a deep and sincere effort to contact Him by study and meditation. If we don't find the pearl of God's presence in one or two divings, we must not blame the ocean; blame our diving. That is what is meant by the science of religion. We must not attach too much importance to the things of this life. We don't know when we will have to leave them; that proves that it is foolish to waste time on them.

You are not a mortal being. You are made in the image of God. Never let anyone call you a sinner. No matter what you were yesterday, you are a child of God now and evermore. You must scientifically seek Him. Isn't it worthwhile to forsake small gifts for the greater gift of God? Before meditation, say, "One by one I close the doors of the senses, lest the aroma of the rose or the song of the nightingale distract my love from Thee." Meditation is proof of the existence of God.

The joy that you are seeking in sex, money, wine, human love, or fame is within yourself. Everything you want and need is within you. Seek long and seek deeply. Make up your mind that no one is going to distract you, then you won't be aware of the passing of time. That is the way to make religion scientific. Jesus had the power to destroy the world, but instead he said, "Father, forgive them, for they know not what they do." This shows that the law of God allowed Jesus to go through suffering in order to prove how God wants His saints to live.

If I can convince you that the path of meditation and the search for God lead to everlasting life, then I have given you more than a million dollars, because a million dollars will perish from the earth, but this teaching will go with you beyond the portals of the grave. Be regular in long meditation and be persistent. Forget your body and your thoughts. Between your restless thought and God there is a wall, and many people never surmount that wall, but the fighter goes on. When your mind becomes quiet, you are in the kingdom of the Infinite.

The joy of God is boundless and ever-new. You will find everything and understand everything in God. India's spiritual Masters always teach students to first seek God, then God will reveal all things to them. Behind all earthly mothers there is One Mother; behind all friends, One Friend; behind all fathers, One Father; behind all loves, One Love.

BECOME A YOGI

A yogi is not a sword-swallower, crystal gazer, or snake charmer, but one who knows the scientific psycho-physical technique of uniting the matter-bound body and soul with their source of origin, the Blessed Spirit.

He is a yogi who says: "I shall go within to bring Thee without. Where I am Thou must come."

Such an enlightened one dives deep within the soul through meditation, and brings God-realization without to apply it in worldly life. He is a Yogi who acts for all, and not he who shirks activity or is a fugitive from the battle of life. If we all go to the forest, we will have to build a city there and face the problems of life just the same.

A business man, literary man, artist, musician, laborer, or king; all can be yogis, if they so choose.

A yogi aspires to know the Spirit through living according to the spiritual laws of life, thru renunciation of all material fruits of success and by devoting such fruits to the good of all. Such a man as the Hershey chocolate king, who has given his entire fortune of eighty million to a school, and now works in his own factory, has accomplished renunciation equal to that of great saints.

We must struggle to attain success and have the broadening experiences of life. Many would-be yogis say, "My wife died, I lost my wealth; hence I will forsake everything and become a hermit." Why, they have nothing to forsake! Such sacrifice is not real. It is the renunciation of the fruits of successful action, the translation of selfish ambition into selfless service for all, that is true sacrifice.

Remember that you are made in His image

God made us in His image, but when a little disturbance comes, we forget that image. As we meditate more, the image of God will become predominant and we will lose the image of Satan. Our tests are only to show us that we are Spirit.

Never give up. Earth-life is not perfect. It is a test of our spiritual existence. We must be able to behold the image of God all the time. It is a negative state of existence when we forget the vast image of God within us.

The physical body is a dream, and death is a dream. So, every time you are in trouble, just say, "I am dreaming." Nothing can really happen to you. That is the ultimate realization; just one dream happening to other dreams. The big fish eats the little fish; both are dreams.

Death is not a punishment; it is an awakening; it is a release. We cry for a loved one, saying, "How terrible! He is gone." Still, we are the ones to be pitied. One great Swami in India said, "Insult not my death with your pity, ye who are left on this desolate shore still to mourn and deplore. It is I who pity you."

Having a lot of material things is not happiness. Security of existence is happiness. You must contact God. Having Him, you will know that you have everything in the material world and in the hereafter as well.

Only those who are interested in God can tell you about Him. Remember, you are alone in the world. You came alone and will leave alone. God has given you certain duties which you must perform, but that does not mean that you should forget Him. Serve the family in which you were born, but serve the bigger family of the world, and serve God above all, because you cannot do anything without the power borrowed from Him.

Why do you think that this life is so important when you may be called away in a second?

Material entanglements, sweet and mysterious, keep us dreaming so that we forget to wake up before the dream of Life vanishes into the Infinite. When you have ample time, steadiness, good health, and determination, then wavering suspicions and doubts are walls in the way. They have to be dynamited by Fate before the lotus leaves of our lives wither and let the dewdrops of consciousness slip into the ocean of Oblivion before awakening an expansion into God.

RECEIVE THE MAGNETISM OF A SAINT OR GURU

When a magnet is rubbed against a piece of non-magnetic iron or steel, the latter also becomes magnetic. People, too, can become magnetized through close association with magnetic personalities to whom they give their deep, loving, respectful attention.

If a man continuously thinks, dreams, and visualizes the qualities he desires, and concentrates upon the visual image and mentalities of persons possessing these qualities, he can develop that magnetism from within.

In case of exchanging moral, mental, aesthetic, and spiritual magnetism, immediate contact is not always necessary. Such magnetism can be derived from a distance by meditating upon different persons' visual images and mentalities — possessing different magnetisms. For instance, one who deeply meditates upon the image and mentality of a spiritual man attracts his nature and imitates his spiritual magnetism.

When electricity passes through a wire it becomes magnetic — so, also, if a man continuously thinks, lives, and dreams on morality, aesthetic objects, spirituality, and friendship, he can develop moral, aesthetic, and spiritual magnetism from within.

The most important reason for having a guru is stated in the Bible itself. It says there, "But as many as received him, to them gave he power to become the sons of God."

The guru gives his disciple not only teaching and guidance: He also transmits to him spiritual power. As Jesus raised Lazarus from the dead, so the guru raises the disciple inwardly to the life of the Spirit. The Lord Himself, through the guru, awakens the devotee from his age-old sleep of delusion.

Yogis teach that a disciple is spiritually magnetized by reverent contact with a master; a subtle current is generated. The devotee's undesirable habit-mechanisms in the brain are often cauterized; the groove of his worldly tendencies beneficially disturbed. Momentarily at least he may find the secret veils of *maya* lifting, and glimpse the reality of bliss.

By attracting to yourself the guru's realization of God, you attain his state of Self-realization.

One attracts spiritual teachers when he is desirous of spiritual training, but a guru, or direct messenger of God, is sent only when the disciple is extremely determined to

know God. God uses the speech, mind, and wisdom of
the guru to teach and redeem the disciple.

DEDICATE YOURSELF TO FINDING GOD

We read about God in the various scriptures. We hear
of His presence and hear Him praised in the sermons of
religious men and saints. We imagine Him behind the
veils of beauty in Nature. We think about His existence
through the logic within us. But all of these windows
through which we try to see God are fitted with the
opaque glass of uncertain inference drawn from untested,
unscrutinized data.

God's light can never shine through the closed doors
of blind sentiment. Through the open window of logical
seeking God may be found. Satisfaction in a belief about
God without actually contacting Him is the death of wisdom and divine acquaintanceship. Do not remain idle
and hidden behind the cloak of a denominational religion and thus cease making a real effort to know God in
this life.

The great proof of the existence of God can only be found within, by deeply, daily practicing some right method of meditation. Find Him within, and you will find Him not only in the holiest of holy places, but you will find Him everywhere. One hour of deep meditation will make you feel truth more than a lifetime of theoretical study of scriptures.

When your mind is free from prejudice, when narrow-mindedness vanishes, when you unreservedly sympathize with everybody, when you hear the voice of God in the chorus of churches, tabernacles, temples, and mosques, when you realize that life is a joyous battle of duty, and at the same time a passing dream, and, above all, when you become increasingly intoxicated with the joy of meditation and in making others happy by giving them God-Peace, then you will know that God is with you always, and you are in Him.

Never mind if first you cannot see God or hear His knock at the gate of your heart. For a long time you have been hiding from Him and running away in the marsh of the senses. It is the noise of your own rowdy passions and of the flight of your heavy footsteps in the material world that has made you unable to hear His call within. Stop, be calm, pray steadfastly, and out of the silence will loom forth the Divine Presence.

Affirmation

He who rubs his soul

on the Divine Magnet

by concentration,

becomes a part of that Magnet, God,

and he attracts to himself all that is good.

Appendix

Yogananda's *Energization Exercises*: 20 body part recharging*

The *Energization Exercises* are not ordinary physical exercises. They are a spiritual technique of *pranayama*, or life-force control.

- On the physical level, by increasing the flow of life-force (prana) you will keep your body in a magnetic state of increased health.

- On a mental level that stronger flow will result in a growing sense of positivity, will power, and magnetism.

- On the spiritual level the training to consciously control the life force will prepare you for the deeper yogic practices, for true *pranayama*, during meditation.

If you practice with awareness, you will gradually learn to perceive the energy in the body. In time you will consider yourself not only a bundle of flesh and bones, but as a being of energy.

* The entire series of the 39 *Energization Exercises* can be learned at any Ananda center or through the *Energization Exercises Booklet* by Crystal Clarity Publishers.

The *Energization Exercises* also teach you how to tap into the cosmic Source of energy, through the medulla oblongata. Eventually you will feel your daily life being completely transformed: you will live not only by your personal power, but will become a magnetic channel of a higher, cosmic flow, as you speak, work, think, interact.

How to practice

Start by invoking the Cosmic Energy:
  "O Infinite Spirit,
  recharge my body with Thy cosmic energy;
  my mind with concentration;
  and my soul with Thy ever-new joy.
  O eternal youth of body and mind,
  abide in me forever and forever."

To obtain maximum results, perform each exercise with deepest concentration and will power.

Keep the eyes closed and focused upward at the point between the eyebrows, the spiritual eye. This is the center of will in man. Will is the power that operates the floodgate of the medulla oblongata (seated at the back of the neck), which is the principal point of entry of cosmic energy into the body.

By keeping the eyes focused at the spiritual eye, and visualizing the cosmic energy flowing into the body through the medulla oblongata, a direct connection is established between the will and the flow of life energy.

Visualize the cosmic energy entering the body through the medulla oblongata, and direct it, by your will power, to the body part that you are exercising. Direct the energy to the center of that body part.

In tensing each body part, always remember to start with a low degree of tension, progressing to medium, then to high tension, and finally vibrate. Then relax from high to medium to low tension, to complete relaxation.

Don't tense with a quick or jerky motion. Never exert tension to the point of strain or discomfort.

Apply these two principles

"The stronger the will, the stronger the flow of energy."

"Tense with will, relax and feel."

20 Body Part Recharging Technique

1) Inhaling gradually tense the entire body simultaneously. Hold the tension for a count of three, filling it with energy; then exhale and relax gradually.

2) Then tense the following twenty body parts individually, directing energy to each part, one by one:
   Left foot, right foot, left calf, right calf, left thigh, right thigh, left buttock, right buttock, abdomen (below navel), stomach (above navel), left forearm, right forearm, left upper arm, right upper arm, left chest, right chest, left of neck, right of neck, front of neck, back of neck.

3) Now tense the same body-parts, one after the other, but this time maintain a medium tension in each body part. When all muscles are tensed (filled with energy), relax one muscle at a time in reverse order.

4) Repeat the first phase, bringing the chin to the chest.

THE *HONG-SAU* TECHNIQUE
OF MEDITATION

(From Yogananda's original Praecepta Lessons)

1. Sit erect on edge of bed with feet on floor, or sit on a cushioned chair, or sit on a bed with your legs crossed*, facing East, with spine straight, chest out, abdomen in, shoulder blades together, chin parallel to the ground, and up-turned, cup-shaped palms resting at the junction of the abdomen and thighs.

2. Then precede the actual practice of the *Hong-Sau* Technique with an awakening prayer, which coincides with your desire or purpose of concentration; as, for example, for wisdom, peace, and contentment, repeat the following prayer:

> "Heavenly Father, Jesus Christ, Saints of all religions, the Spirit in my body temple, Supreme Master Minds of India, Supreme Master Babaji, Great Master Lahiri Mahasaya, Master Swami Sri Yukteswar Giriji, and Guru-Preceptor, I bow to you all. Lead me from ignorance to wisdom; from restlessness to peace; from desires to contentment."

* You may also sit on a cushion or bench.

3. Inhale slowly, counting 1 to 20. Hold the breath, counting 1 to 20. Then exhale slowly, counting 1 to 20*. Repeat this 6 to 12 times. Tense the whole body, clenching the fists. Relax the whole body, throwing the breath out. Repeat 6 times.

4. Then exhale quickly, and remain without breath as long as it will stay out without discomfort, and mentally wait for the breath to come in. When the breath comes in of itself, mentally say *HONG*, and when the breath goes out of itself, mentally say, *SAU*. Keep the eyes closed or open without winking or gazing, and gently fixed upward on the point between the eyebrows.

5. After practicing this technique deeply for ten minutes to one-half an hour, exhale slowly and completely. Blow all the breath out of the lungs which you possibly can, and enjoy the breathless state as long as you can without discomfort. Repeat three times. Then forget the breath and pray, or sit in Silence.

---

* Use a lesser count, if necessary, like 8-8-8 and gradually lengthen it over time.

Follow these instructions

Long concentration must be preceded by 15 minutes' practice of the *Energization Exercises.** By faithfully practicing this technique ... and by longer meditations in the morning and at night, and also a three-hour meditation once a week, on any day suitable to you, you will find that you will be well advanced in the spiritual path.

In the morning, this *Hong-Sau* technique should be practiced after the *Energization Exercises.* You must get used to the practicing of this technique with your eyes gently concentrated upon the point between the eyebrows. Do not strain the eyes. However, if you are not used to holding the eyes in this position, practice some of the time with your eyes half open, but most of the time with eyes closed. You can practice with eyes closed, and in leisure hours lie down on your back, and watch the breath, mentally chanting *Hong-Sau.* The more you practice in your leisure hours, the greater will be the results. Work overtime and you will gain still better results.

When you consciously watch the breath, what happens? The heart, the lungs, and the diaphragm gradually calm down and their muscles ultimately, during a long

---

* For now, you may practice the 20-body part recharging which you find in this book.

deep silence, refrain from constant motion. Thus, decay is stopped throughout the system, and then no more venous blood has to be pumped by the heart into the lungs. When the heart does not pump blood, the lungs do not expand any more to receive more oxygen; then you do not breathe any more. When this happens, decay is stopped entirely. When decay is stopped, you no longer are in need of new, red blood, oxygen, nor food — but can live directly from Cosmic Energy running through the medulla, and not by the energy distilled from food only.

It is always a good plan to exhale and drive away the poisons before beginning deep breathing. By practicing the inhalation and exhalation exercises, the carbon in the venous blood is burned out and partial decay is stopped in the body. You will notice that when you throw the breath out after practicing this technique for a long time and deeply, that you have no desire to breathe for a long time. You can remain longer in the breathless state than if you tried breathlessness immediately after restlessness.

Be conscious of inhalation and exhalation

1. In doing the above, do not force the breath in and out. Breathe naturally, only watch the course of the incoming

and outgoing breath, mentally chanting *Hong* and *Sau*. If the breath naturally stops in the lungs or outside, wait until it flows again of itself.

2. Remember that the purpose of this practice is to *increase naturally the intervals when the breath does not flow*. If the breath goes in of itself and does not flow out immediately, wait and enjoy the state of breathlessness. When it comes out again, say *Sau*. If the breath goes out and stays out, wait and enjoy that state of breathlessness, until the breath wants to flow in again.

3. The breath is first thrown out so that you may know when to begin mentally chanting *Hong* when the breath goes in. In ordinary breathing you are not aware whether the breath is in or out.

4. Do not force the breath in and out in order to chant. Let the mental chant follow the natural desire of the breath to flow in and out.

5. Concentrate upon the intervals when the breath does not flow, without forcing this quiet breathless state.

6. By watching the breath, *you metaphysically destroy the identification of the soul with the breath and the body*. By watching the breath, you separate your Ego from it and know that your body exists only partially by breath.

7. By watching the breath, what happens? When you first tense and relax the outer body and throw out the breath, you have removed motion and decay from the outward muscles, but not from the internal organs — heart, lungs, diaphragm, and so on. By watching the breath, breathing becomes rhythmic and calm. Watching of the breath calms and quiets the heart. A restless and worried mind increases heart action, and a quiet mind calms the heart action. A heaving breath also increases heart action and quiet breath calms the heart. By watching the breath calmly, both the breath and the mind become calm. A calm mind and breath slow down and quiet the motion of the heart, diaphragm, and lungs.

When the motion is simultaneously removed (1) from the muscles by relaxation and by casting out the breath, (2) and from the inner organs, heart, lungs, diaphragm, and so on, then the Life Energy, which is used to pump 18 tons of blood through the heart in 24 hours, retires to the spine and becomes distributed in the billions of body cells. This energy electrifies the cells and prevents their decay, making them self-sustained dry batteries. In such a state the cells do not require oxygen or food chemicals to sustain life. It is in this state that the vitalized cells do not need to repair decay, because when decay is removed from outer and inner organs the venous blood does not become impure and it does not need to be sent to the heart to be pumped into the lungs to be purified by the incoming oxygen in the breath.

ABOUT THE AUTHOR

PARAMHANSA YOGANANDA

"As a bright light shining in the midst of darkness, so was Yogananda's presence in this world. Such a great soul comes on earth only rarely, when there is a real need among men."

—His Holiness the Shankaracharya of Kanchipuram

Born in 1893, Yogananda was the first yoga master of India to take up permanent residence in the West.

Yogananda arrived in America in 1920 and traveled throughout the country on what he called his "spiritual campaigns." Hundreds of thousands filled the largest halls in major cities to see the yoga master from India. Yogananda continued to lecture and write up to his passing in 1952.

Yogananda's initial impact on Western culture was truly impressive. His lasting spiritual legacy has been even greater. His *Autobiography of a Yogi*, first published in 1946, helped launch a spiritual revolution in the West. Translated into more than fifty languages, it remains a best-selling spiritual classic to this day.

Before embarking on his mission, Yogananda received this admonition from his teacher, Swami Sri Yukteswar: "The West is high in material attainments but lacking in spiritual understanding. It is God's will that you play a role in teaching mankind the value of balancing the material with an inner, spiritual life."

In addition to *Autobiography of a Yogi*, Yogananda's spiritual legacy includes music, poetry, and extensive commentaries on the Bhagavad Gita, the *Rubaiyat* of Omar Khayyam, and the Christian Bible, showing the principles of Self-realization as the unifying truth underlying all true religions. Through his teachings and his Kriya Yoga path millions of people around the world have found a new way to connect personally with God.

His mission, however, was far broader than all this. It was to help usher the whole world into Dwapara Yuga, the new Age of Energy in which we live. "Someday," Swami Kriyananda wrote, "I believe he will be seen as the *avatar* of Dwapara Yuga: the way shower for a new age."

Further Explorations

CRYSTAL CLARITY PUBLISHERS

If you enjoyed this title, Crystal Clarity Publishers invites you to deepen your spiritual life through many additional resources based on the teachings of Paramhansa Yogananda. We offer books, e-books, audiobooks, yoga and meditation videos, and a wide variety of inspirational and relaxation music composed by Swami Kriyananda.

See a listing of books below, visit our secure website for a complete online catalog, or place an order for our products.

crystalclarity.com

800.424.1055 | clarity@crystalclarity.com

1123 Goodrich Blvd. | Commerce, CA 90022

ANANDA WORLDWIDE

Crystal Clarity Publishers is the publishing house of Ananda, a worldwide spiritual movement founded by Swami Kriyananda, a direct disciple of Paramhansa Yogananda. Ananda offers resources and support for your spiritual journey through meditation instruction, webinars, online virtual community, email, and chat.

Ananda has more than 150 centers and meditation groups in over 45 countries, offering group guided meditations, classes and teacher training in meditation and yoga, and many other resources.

In addition, Ananda has developed eight residential communities in the US, Europe, and India. Spiritual communities are places where people live together in a spirit of cooperation and friendship, dedicated to a common goal. Spirituality is practiced in all areas of daily life: at school, at work, and in the home. Many Ananda communities offer internships during which one can stay and experience spiritual community firsthand.

For more information about Ananda communities or meditation groups near you, please visit ananda.org or call 530.478.7560.

THE EXPANDING LIGHT RETREAT

The Expanding Light is the largest retreat center in the world to share exclusively the teachings of Paramhansa Yogananda. Situated in the Ananda Village community near Nevada City, California, the center offers the opportunity to experience spiritual life in a contemporary ashram setting. The varied, year-round schedule of classes and programs on yoga, meditation, and spiritual practice includes Karma Yoga, personal retreat, spiritual travel, and online learning. Large groups are welcome.

The Ananda School of Yoga & Meditation offers certified yoga, spiritual counselor, and meditation teacher trainings.

The teaching staff has years of experience practicing Kriya Yoga meditation and all aspects of Paramhansa Yogananda's teachings. You may come for a relaxed personal renewal, participating in ongoing activities as much or as little as you wish. The serene mountain setting, supportive staff, and delicious vegetarian meals provide an ideal environment for a truly meaningful stay, be it a brief respite or an extended spiritual vacation.

For more information, please visit expandinglight.org or call 800.346.5350.

ANANDA MEDITATION RETREAT

Set amidst seventy-two acres of beautiful meditation gardens and wild forest in Northern California's Sierra foothills, the Ananda Meditation Retreat is an ideal setting for a rejuvenating, inner experience.

The Meditation Retreat has been a place of deep meditation and sincere devotion for over fifty years. Long before that, the Native American Maidu tribe held this to be sacred land. The beauty and presence of the Divine are tangibly felt by all who visit here.

Studies show that being in nature and using techniques such as forest bathing can significantly reduce stress and blood pressure while strengthening your immune system, concentration, and level of happiness. The Meditation Retreat is the perfect place for quiet immersion in nature.

Plan a personal retreat, enjoy one of the guided retreats, or choose from a variety of programs led by the caring and joyful staff.

For more information or to place your reservation, please visit meditationretreat.org, email meditationretreat@ananda.org, or call 530.478.7557.

The WISDOM of YOGANANDA series

The Wisdom of Yogananda series features writings of Paramhansa Yogananda not available elsewhere. Presented with minimal editing, these books capture the Master's expansive and compassionate wisdom, his sense of fun, and his practical spiritual guidance. The books include writings from his earliest years in America, offering timeless wisdom in an approachable, easy-to-read format. Yogananda is a fresh and original voice and one of the most highly regarded spiritual teachers of the twentieth century.

HOW TO BE HAPPY ALL THE TIME

The Wisdom of Yogananda, Volume 1

Yogananda explains everything needed to lead a happier, more fulfilling life. Topics include: looking for happiness in the right places; choosing to be happy; tools, techniques, and methods for achieving happiness; sharing happiness with others; and balancing success with happiness.

KARMA AND REINCARNATION

The Wisdom of Yogananda, Volume 2

Yogananda reveals the reality of karma, death, reincarnation, and the afterlife. With clarity and simplicity, he makes the mysterious understandable: why we see a world of suffering and inequality; what happens at death and after death; the purpose of reincarnation; and how to handle the challenges we face in our lives.

HOW TO LOVE AND BE LOVED

The Wisdom of Yogananda, Volume 3

Yogananda shares practical guidance and fresh insight on relationships of all types: how to cure friendship-ending habits; how to choose the right partner; the role of sex in marriage; how to conceive a spiritually oriented child; the solutions to problems that arise in marriage; and the Universal Love at the heart of all relationships.

HOW TO BE A SUCCESS

The Wisdom of Yogananda, Volume 4

The Attributes of Success, Yogananda's original booklet on reaching one's goals, is included here along with his other writings on success: how to develop habits of success and eradicate habits of failure; thriving in the right job; how to build willpower and magnetism; and finding the true purpose of one's life.

HOW TO HAVE COURAGE, CALMNESS, AND CONFIDENCE

The Wisdom of Yogananda, Volume 5

A master at helping people change and grow, Yogananda shows how to transform one's life: dislodge negative thoughts and depression; uproot fear and thoughts of failure; cure nervousness and systematically eliminate worry from life; and overcome anger, sorrow, oversensitivity, and a host of other troublesome emotions.

Winner of the 2011 International Book Award for Best Self-Help Title

HOW TO ACHIEVE GLOWING HEALTH AND VITALITY

The Wisdom of Yogananda, Volume 6

Yogananda explains principles that promote physical health and overall well-being, mental clarity, and inspiration in one's spiritual life. He offers practical, wide-ranging, and fascinating suggestions on having more energy and living a radiantly healthy life. Readers will discover the priceless Energization Exercises for rejuvenating the body and mind, the fine art of conscious relaxation, and helpful diet tips for health and beauty.

HOW TO AWAKEN YOUR TRUE POTENTIAL

The Wisdom of Yogananda, Volume 7

With compassion, humor, and deep understanding of human psychology, Yogananda offers instruction on releasing limitations to access the power of mind and heart. Discover your hidden resources and be empowered to choose a life with greater meaning, purpose, and joy.

THE MAN WHO REFUSED HEAVEN

The Wisdom of Yogananda, Volume 8

Why is humor so deeply appreciated? Laughter is one of the great joys of life. Joy is fundamental to who we are. The humor in this book is taken from Yogananda's writings. Also included are experiences with the Master that demonstrate his playful spirit.

HOW TO FACE LIFE'S CHANGES

The Wisdom of Yogananda, Volume 9

Changes come not to destroy us, but to help us grow and learn the lessons we must to reach our highest potential. Guided by Yogananda, tap into the changeless joy of your soul-nature, empowering you to move through life fearlessly, with an open heart. Learn to accept change as the reality of life; face change in relationships, finances, and health with gratitude; and cultivate key attitudes like fearlessness, non-attachment, and willpower.

HOW TO SPIRITUALIZE YOUR LIFE

The Wisdom of Yogananda, Volume 10

Yogananda answers a wide range of questions from truth seekers, sharing his teachings and insights on how to be successful in the everyday world and in one's spiritual life. Addressing financial, physical, mental, emotional, and spiritual challenges, he explains how best to expand one's consciousness and live life to the fullest. Compiled from his articles, lessons, and handwritten letters, this tenth volume is well suited to both individual and group study.

HOW TO LIVE WITHOUT FEAR

The Wisdom of Yogananda, Volume 11

Yogananda said that one of the greatest enemies of willpower is fear. Avoid it both in thought and in action. Fear doesn't help you to get away from the object of fear, it only paralyzes your willpower. Here Yogananda, teaches us how to: eliminate the mental bacteria of fear, rid the mind of worry poisons, overcome stage fright, use chants and affirmations to overcome fear, and much more!

SCIENTIFIC HEALING AFFIRMATIONS

Paramhansa Yogananda

This reprint of the original 1924 classic by Paramhansa Yogananda is a pioneering work in the fields of self-healing and self-transformation. He explains that words are crystallized thoughts and have life-changing power when spoken with conviction, concentration, willpower, and feeling. Yogananda offers far more than mere suggestions for achieving positive attitudes. He shows how to impregnate words with spiritual force to shift habitual thought patterns of the mind and create a new personal reality.

Added to this text are over fifty of Yogananda's well-loved "Short Affirmations," taken from issues of *East-West* and *Inner Culture* magazines from 1932 to 1942. This little book will be a treasured companion.

METAPHYSICAL MEDITATIONS

Paramhansa Yogananda

Metaphysical Meditations is a classic collection of meditation techniques, visualizations, affirmations, and prayers from the great yoga master, Paramhansa Yogananda. The meditations given are of three types: those spoken to the individual consciousness, prayers or demands addressed to God, and affirmations that bring us closer to the Divine.

Select a passage that meets your specific need and speak each word slowly and purposefully until you become absorbed in its inner meaning. At the bedside, by the meditation seat, or while traveling — one can choose no better companion than *Metaphysical Meditations*.

SONGS OF THE SOUL

Paramhansa Yogananda

Yogananda preferred to express his wisdom not in dry intellectual terms but as pure, expansive feeling. To drink his poetry is to be drawn into the web of his boundless, childlike love. In one moment his *Songs of the Soul* invite us to join him as he plays among the stars with his Cosmic Beloved. Then they call us to discover that portion of our own hearts that is eternally one with the Nearest and Dearest. This volume is a bubbling, singing wellspring of spiritual healing that we can bring with us everywhere.

WHISPERS FROM ETERNITY

A Book of Answered Prayers
Paramhansa Yogananda
Edited by his disciple, Swami Kriyananda

Many poetic works can inspire, but few have the power to change lives. These poems and prayers have been "spiritualized" by Paramhansa Yogananda: Each has drawn a response from the Divine. Yogananda was not only a master poet whose imagery here is still as vivid and alive as when first published in 1949: He was a spiritual master, an avatar.

He encouraged his disciples to read from *Whispers from Eternity* every day, explaining that through these verses, he could guide them after his passing. But this book is not for his disciples alone. It is for spiritual aspirants of any tradition who wish to drink from this bountiful fountain of pure inspiration and wisdom.

The Original 1946 Unedited Edition of Yogananda's Spiritual Masterpiece

AUTOBIOGRAPHY OF A YOGI

Paramhansa Yogananda

Autobiography of a Yogi is one of the world's most acclaimed spiritual classics, with millions of copies sold. Named one of the Best 100 Spiritual Books of the twentieth century, this book helped launch and continues to inspire a spiritual awakening throughout the Western world.

Yogananda was the first yoga master of India whose mission brought him to live and teach in the West. His firsthand account of his life experiences in India includes childhood revelations, stories of his visits to saints and masters, and long-secret teachings of yoga and self-realization that he first made available to the Western reader.

This reprint of the original 1946 edition is free from textual changes made after Yogananda's passing in 1952. This updated edition includes bonus materials: the last chapter that Yogananda wrote in 1951, also without posthumous changes, the eulogy Yogananda wrote for Gandhi, and a new foreword and afterword by Swami Kriyananda, one of Yogananda's close, direct disciples.

Also available in Spanish and Hindi from Crystal Clarity Publishers.

More about Paramhansa Yogananda

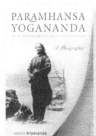

PARAMHANSA YOGANANDA

A Biography with Personal Reflections and
Reminiscences
Swami Kriyananda

Paramhansa Yogananda's life was filled with aston-
ishing accomplishments. And yet in his classic autobiography, he wrote more about the saints he'd met
than about his own spiritual attainments. Yogananda's
direct disciple, Swami Kriyananda, relates the untold
story of this great master and world teacher: his teenage miracles, his
challenges in coming to America, his national lecture campaigns, his
struggles to fulfill his world-changing mission amid incomprehension
and painful betrayals, and his ultimate triumphant achievement.

Kriyananda's subtle grasp of his guru's inner nature and outward mission reveals Yogananda's many-sided greatness. Includes many never-be-
fore-published anecdotes and an insider's view of the Master's last years.

THANK YOU, MASTER

Direct Disciples Remember Paramhansa Yogananda
Hare Krishna Ghosh, Meera Ghosh, Peggy Deitz

Anyone who has read and loved *Autobiography of a
Yogi* will be delighted to find this treasure of personal
experiences and heartfelt remembrances of Paramhansa
Yogananda by three of his direct disciples.

Stories from Yogananda's family members, Hare Krishna Ghosh
and Meera Ghosh, who became disciples as teenagers, take the reader
on pilgrimage to India to the sacred places and miraculous moments
shared with this great yogi. The stories of Peggy Deitz transport one to
Yogananda's ashram in California and his life with devotees in America.

Whether humorous or miraculous, mundane or divine, these accounts bring to life the experience of being in Yogananda's presence. They give insight into the profound love with which he guided each individual.

Firsthand experiences from close disciples are a true gift that can help us tune in to his vast nature. At the same time, these delightful stories will touch your heart and uplift your spirit.

THE NEW PATH

My Life with Paramhansa Yogananda
Swami Kriyananda

Winner of the 2010 Eric Hoffer Award for Best Self-Help/Spiritual Book
Winner of the 2010 USA Book News Award for Best Spiritual Book

The New Path is a moving revelation of one man's search for lasting happiness. After rejecting the false promises offered by modern society, J. Donald Walters found himself (much to his surprise) at the feet of Paramhansa Yogananda, asking to become his disciple. How he got there, trained with the Master, and became Swami Kriyananda make fascinating reading.

The rest of the book is the only full account of what it was like for Swami Kriyananda to live with and be a disciple of that great man of God.

Anyone hungering to learn more about Yogananda will delight in the hundreds of stories of life with a great avatar and the profound lessons they offer. This book is an ideal complement to *Autobiography of a Yogi*.

CONVERSATIONS WITH YOGANANDA

Recorded, compiled, and edited by his disciple
Swami Kriyananda

This is an unparalleled account of Yogananda and his teachings written by one of his foremost disciples. Swami Kriyananda was often present when Yogananda spoke privately with other close disciples, received visitors and answered their questions, and dictated and discussed his writings. He recorded the Master's words, preserving a treasure trove of wisdom that would otherwise have been lost.

These Conversations include not only Yogananda's words as he spoke them, but the added insight of a disciple who spent over fifty years attuning his consciousness to that of his guru.

The collection features nearly five hundred stories, sayings, and insights from the twentieth century's most famous master of yoga, as well as twenty-five photos — nearly all previously unreleased.

THE ESSENCE OF SELF-REALIZATION

The Wisdom of Paramhansa Yogananda
Recorded, compiled, and edited by his disciple, Swami Kriyananda

Filled with lessons, stories, and jewels of wisdom that Paramhansa Yogananda shared only with his closest disciples, this volume is an invaluable guide to the spiritual life carefully organized in twenty main topics.

Great teachers work through their students, and Yogananda was no exception. Swami Kriyananda comments, "After I'd been with him a year and a half, he began urging me to write down the things he was saying during informal conversations." Many of the three hundred sayings presented here are available nowhere else. A must-read for anyone wishing to know more about Yogananda's teachings and to absorb his wisdom.

www.ingramcontent.com/pod-product-compliance
Lightning Source LLC
Chambersburg PA
CBHW081606150425
25103CB00049B/826